Melinda Messenger's Family Cookbook

Delicious recipes for
all the family

Melinda Messenger's Family Cookbook

NEW HOLLAND

First published in the UK in 2010 by
New Holland Publishers (UK) Ltd
London   Cape Town   Sydney   Auckland

Garfield House, 86–88 Edgware Road
London W2 2EA
United Kingdom
www.newhollandpublishers.com

80 McKenzie Street
Cape Town 8001
South Africa

Unit 1, 66 Gibbes Street
Chatswood, NSW 2067
Australia

218 Lake Road
Northcote, Auckland
New Zealand

This book includes reference to recipes including nuts, nut oils and nut derivatives.
Pregnant or nursing mothers, the elderly, young children and babies may be potentially
vulnerable to nut allergies and should therefore avoid nuts, nut oils and nut derivatives.

ISBN 978 184773 732 8

Commissioning editor: Clare Sayer
Production: Laurence Poos
Photographer: Tony Briscoe
Food stylist: Clare Greenstreet
Prop stylist: Jo Harris

10 9 8 7 6 5 4 3 2 1

Reproduction by PDQ Digital Media Solutions Ltd, United Kingdom
Printed and bound in Singapore by Tien Wah Press (PTE) Ltd

Contents

Introduction

Why did I want to write this book?

It all started when I was on a camping trip in the summer with a group of families from my children's school. We were all sitting round the fire late one night having just finished a delicious campfire chilli, when we started talking about all the recipes we had shared between us, not only in our immediate group, but with extended family and friends, from traditional recipes passed down from great-grandmothers to the ordinary parent's take on new and exciting cuisines, such as as Mexican, Indian and Chinese. And so the idea for a book came about. My view with the recipes has been that if my family eat it, love it and ask for second helpings, then it's worthy of a place in the book!

Food is so much more than just sustenance; it brings friends and family together. It's an excuse to celebrate or to catch up or just show someone you care about them. I really think there is something special and magical about a home-cooked meal. Whether you are rustling up a quick mushroom omelette for a simple supper or taking time to prepare a delicious butternut and red onion tart or a mixed berry pavlova, something beautiful goes into a home-cooked meal. Children thrive on it – love.

It's a great shame that with our busy, hectic lives so many of us are letting go of the traditions of cooking at home, tempted as we are by the huge range of ready-prepared, quick-fix foods in the supermarkets. I'm the first to admit that when I fall through the door after a hard day's work, exhausted and with hungry tired children to feed, I don't always feel like preparing and cooking a meal from scratch. So having a few quick and easy solutions for quick meals is essential. I've realized

that with a little bit of forethought and some planning, spending a little time preparing food for your loved ones can be a rewarding experience on many levels. I firmly believe that if your children see you in the kitchen, preparing fresh ingredients, they are more likely to take an interest in what they are eating. Pretty soon they will ask if they can help and one of the most effective ways of getting children to eat good food is to get them to make it themselves. Whether it's mixing up some pancake batter or washing and preparing vegetables, it all adds to their positive food experiences. Just be prepared for your kitchen to be a little messier than usual! Cooking and baking never cease to delight my kids. Morgan loves making omelettes and soups, Flynn likes to make bread and knead dough and Evie loves nothing more than breaking eggs in to flour to make a cake. Cooking is the perfect wet weather activity and is a great way to engage bored children. And the best thing is that we all have something lovely to sit down and enjoy afterwards.

Understanding where our food comes from is really important too and by growing some of your own produce you will give your children a glimpse of nature at work. Get yourself a potato barrel, plant a few carrots and grow tomatoes and lettuce in window boxes – failing that have a few pots of herbs on your kitchen windowsill. There's nothing better than fresh organic produce that you have grown yourself.

Sitting down together to eat is a great bonding experience I find, even when the children are fussing about who wants to sit where or announcing suddenly that they don't like mashed potato (usually Evie). However chaotic, it's still a special time for the family to reconnect at the end of a day, and share all the things that have been going on. We usually play guessing games over dinner to stop the three children squabbling too much – each child picks an animal or famous person and the others have to ask questions to find out what or who they are.

My first interest in cooking came from my Granny, who was born and grew up in India. She married my Grandad in her late twenties and they came to England with three children and a large collection of recipes. Granny went on to have five more children (Mum was the seventh child) so she was a real maternal figure, cooking and providing for her large family – as well as for friends and neighbours. My Mum recalls that there was always something delicious to enjoy. I remember when we would go and visit as children – whatever time of the day or night we arrived there would always be a huge spread of food. Hot onion bhajis, vegetable samosas and an assortment of rice dishes were always on offer, but her trademark dish was her baked Alaska. This marvellous dessert caused endless pondering on how ice cream could go into an oven and not melt. The wonders of childhood!

In the summer we would have barbecues and my aunty Kath would prepare all sorts of delicious dishes, from roasted lamb to marinated fish and beautiful salads. Eating outside for me now is still one of my favourite things. As soon as it's warm enough we have picnics, lunches and barbecues out in the open. From campfire chilli to chicken or vegetable kebabs to toasted marshmallows – everything seems to taste better outside! Cooking and eating outdoors always feels magical – even in winter when the fields were covered in snow, we would take hearty soups and hot chocolate on sledging trips. Food and the great outdoors go together beautifully (and there's no worry about crumbs on the floor either). If you're lucky enough you might be able to forage some of your own food – from mushrooms to blackberries to apples. My children relish these experiences as I did.

It's been such a rewarding experience to gather up my favourite recipes, including all those that have been handed down by my family or passed on to me from good friends and have them all in the one place. I hope you enjoy them as much as we do and that there are many laughs and not too many tears shared over the supper table. Here's to clean plates and happy full bellies.

Breakfast

I know, I know, you've all heard it a thousand times but breakfast really is the most important meal of the day – especially for kids. Processed cereals are all very well but I was amazed when I found out just how much sugar and salt you will find in some brands. So whether it's something healthy and filling before you pack them off to school or a delicious cooked breakfast for the weekend, this chapter may just tempt you to try something new.

Crunchy yogurt fool

I absolutely love fresh raspberries and am always trying to find more way to serve them. This is a lovely summer breakfast dish.

PREP TIME 5 minutes
SERVES 4

450 g (14 oz) natural yogurt
50 g (2 oz) soft brown or
   unrefined cane sugar
225 g (8 oz) fresh raspberries
50 g (2 oz) crunchy muesli or
   granola (see opposite)

1   Tip the yogurt into a large bowl and add the sugar. Whisk gently to give it a nicer texture.

2   Mash the raspberries slightly (I use a fork) and add to the yogurt. Stir gently so you just get a nice swirly effect.

3   Spoon into four pretty glass bowls and top each one with the muesli or granola. Serve immediately.

When raspberries are not in season you might want to try other fruits – apple works brilliantly. Just peel and grate 2 apples and mix with the yogurt.

Homemade superfood granola

This is a really easy one to make and is so much better than the shop-bought versions – for the simple reason that you can put in exactly what you like.

PREP TIME 5 minutes
COOKING TIME 30 minutes
SERVES 8

250 g (9 oz) jumbo oats
3 tbsp pumpkin seeds
3 tbsp sunflower seeds
2 tbsp sesame seeds
2 tbsp poppy seeds
75 g (2½ oz) golden
    raisins/sultanas
75 g (2½ oz) desiccated
    coconut
3 tbsp extra-virgin rapeseed
    oil/sunflower oil
3 tbsp runny honey

To serve
yogurt
blueberries
runny honey

1 Preheat the oven to 180°C/350°F/gas 4.

2 Put the oats, seeds, raisins and coconut in a large bowl and mix well.

3 Mix the oil and honey in a small pan, and heat gently. Pour the honey over the oat mixture and mix until all the ingredients are well combined.

4 Spread the mixture out over a non-stick baking tray and bake for 25–30 minutes, until the oats are golden. Shake the ingredients up or even turn if possible at least twice during cooking and be careful not to overcook. Allow to cool completely before storing in an airtight jar.

5 Spoon the granola into a bowl and top with a generous dollop of yogurt, fresh blueberries and a drizzle of honey.

Tip
Other great topping ideas include peeled satsuma/clementine segments, grated apple and strawberries. If you want to make it even more 'super', try goji berries, hemp seeds, cashew nuts. Nutritionally well worth the effort.

Smoothie heaven

Smoothies are such a great way of getting fresh fruit into your children and we are pretty much addicted to them in our family. I have to confess and say that a good deal of smoothies drunk in our house come from a carton, but we do love to make our own. It's also a great way to deal with fruit that you want to use up, such as bananas that have gone a little brown or strawberries that have been squished. Not all our attempts are smoothie perfection but we are certainly having fun trying. You can also try experimenting with herbs such as basil, mint or sage. This recipe goes down particularly well in our house.

PREP TIME 10 minutes
SERVES 4

large handful of strawberries
small bunch of seedless
   grapes (any colour)
about 4 small apples
3 kiwis
3 bananas
4 large oranges
1 lime

1 First prepare your fruit. Wash and hull the strawberries and grapes, peel and core the apples and cut into small pieces. (Wayne doesn't bother with this bit – he's quite happy to have a few pips thrown in!). Peel the kiwis and bananas and cut into chunks.

2 Put everything in your blender and process until smooth.

3 Squeeze the juice from the oranges and lime and add to the blender. Blend again and then pour into large glasses. Enjoy!

Tip
For a refreshingly chilled smoothie, it's a good idea to keep your fruit in the fridge (except the bananas) before blending. Or simply add a few ice cubes.

Sunny toast

This is something my sister-in-law Tracy taught us a few years back. The kids love it and demand it at least once a month. Anything that requires a little imagination or creativity with shapes creates a little fun that makes the dish even more desirable!

PREP TIME 2 minutes
COOKING TIME 8–10 minutes
SERVES 1

butter
1 slice of wholemeal bread
1 small egg
biscuit/cookie cutters

1 Preheat the oven to 200°C/400°F/gas 6. Grease a baking sheet with a little butter (I use a piece of kitchen towel to rub butter over the tray). You can use margarine or oil if you prefer.

2 Spread butter onto one side of your sliced bread. Then, press your shape cutter into the centre of the bread to make a hole. Ours are flower-shaped for Evie and gingerbread men for the boys. Just make sure that you can cut out a shape big enough to pour an egg into.

3 Take out the shape you have cut. Then, place the slice on your baking tray with the buttered side facing up. We place the cut-out shape on the tray as well.

4 Break the egg onto a small plate or saucer and use the plate to slide your egg into the hole in your bread.

5 Place the tray into the pre-heated oven and bake for around 8 minutes. (Morgan likes his less runny so his stays in for 10 minutes.)

6 When your sunny toast is ready, use a spatula or something similar to slide onto your plates.

Perfect porridge

Whether it's for adults or children, porridge is just about unbeatable when it comes to having a good start to the day. Oats have a low glycaemic index, which means they are digested slowly giving a steady rise in blood glucose levels. Result: its slow energy release will keep you going well past lunchtime. Besides, is there a better start to a cold winter's day, than warming your hands around a hot bowl of porridge?

PREP TIME 2 minutes
COOKING TIME 10 minutes
SERVES 4–5

1.2 litres (2 pints) semi-
   skimmed milk
175 g (6 oz) porridge oats
1 tbsp unrefined cane
   sugar
pinch salt
sprinkle of sugar, to serve

1 Set 250 ml (9 fl oz) of milk aside and place the rest in a large, non-stick pan. Bring slowly to the boil.

2 Stir in the oats, sugar and salt and reduce the heat to very low. Cook for 8 minutes, stirring often.

3 When you are ready to serve, add the remaining milk and stir until warm again, but not boiling. This seems to make it a much creamier porridge. Pour into warm bowls and sprinkle over a little sugar just to make it sparkle! The porridge is now ready for your favourite toppings!

Tip
The most important rule of all in making good porridge is to not let it burn or stick to the pan. The key here is to reduce to a very low heat and cook slowly for a few minutes longer.

Serving suggestions

Let's be honest, almost anyone can cook it; the fun is then fine-tuning it to your requirements. My family is a great example of why you need to have options, I make a huge pan full for everyone but I will lay the breakfast table with all sorts of porridge paraphernalia. Here are some of the most popular choices:

Evie – a swirl of golden syrup; Flynn – a big dollop of strawberry jam; Morgan – just a sprinkle of brown sugar on the top (the traditional option!); Wayne – Manuka honey and some fresh fruit such as blueberries. I like chopped banana, dried apricots and a pinch of ground cinnamon.

Cranberry and sesame brunch bars

These delicious brunch bars are really easy to make and are full of goodness too. Make them in advance and have the perfect morning snack when you are pressed for time.

PREP TIME 10 minutes
COOKING TIME 20 minutes
MAKES 10–12 bars

250 g (9 oz) rolled oats
75 g (2½ oz) almonds, finely chopped
75 g (2½ oz) raisins
125 g (4½ oz) dried cranberries
50 g (2 oz) sesame seeds
150 g (5½ oz) butter
200 g (7 oz) Demerara sugar
125 g (4½ oz) runny honey

1 Preheat the oven to 190°C/375°F/gas 5. Grease and line a 20 x 30 cm (8 x 12 in) baking tin with greaseproof paper.

2 Pour the oats, almonds, raisins, dried cranberries and sesame seeds into a large bowl. Mix together, making sure all the ingredients are combined.

3 Put the butter, sugar and honey in a pan and place over a low heat. Stir gently for a couple of minutes until the sugar has completely melted. Allow to cool slightly.

4 Pour the mix over the dry ingredients and carefully mix through. Transfer to your prepared tin and press gently to the edges.

5 Bake in the oven for approximately 20 minutes or until golden. Allow to cool and when it is completely cold place in the refrigerator for a further 2 hours. Turn out onto a chopping board and cut into bars.

These will keep for about a week if kept in an airtight container – but I don't imagine they will be around for that long!

American-style pancakes

Who doesn't love pancakes? Flat and thin or slightly thicker like these American-style ones, they make a great breakfast treat.

PREP TIME 6 minutes
COOKING TIME 10 minutes
SERVES 4

110 g (4 oz) self-raising flour
2 tbsp caster sugar
1 tsp bicarbonate of soda
1 egg
25 g (1 oz) butter, melted
300 ml (10 fl oz) buttermilk
oil or butter, for frying
maple syrup
100 g (3½ oz) blueberries
2 large bananas sliced
natural yogurt, crème fraîche,
  cream or ice cream to serve

1 Sieve together the flour, sugar and bicarbonate of soda into a large mixing bowl and make a well in the centre.

2 In a separate bowl mix together the egg, butter and buttermilk. Pour this mixture into the well in the dry ingredients, adding a little at a time and stirring to draw in the flour from the sides of the bowl. Mix until you have a smooth batter.

3 Heat a large frying pan and wipe with a little oil or melted butter (I use a kitchen towel for this). Pour spoonfuls of the batter into the pan and cook for a couple of minutes on each side. Use a spatula or palette knife to turn them over – they should be nicely golden. Cook in batches – you can keep the pancakes warm by covering with a clean cloth and placing in a low oven.

4 Arrange your pancakes on a platter and drizzle over the maple syrup. You could also try runny honey – some floral honeys have a wonderful flavour. Scatter over the fresh fruit and serve with a pot of natural organic yogurt, crème fraîche, squirty cream or even ice cream!

French toast

A gorgeous and delicious alternative to your morning toast.

PREP TIME 2 minutes
COOKING TIME 5 minutes
SERVES 4

4 eggs
125 ml (4½ fl oz) milk
2 tbsp sugar
1 tsp vanilla essence
   (ground cinnamon also
   tastes great)
½ tsp salt
butter, for frying
8 slices white bread
caster sugar and strawberries,
   to serve

1 Beat the eggs with the milk and sugar and pour into a shallow dish. Add the vanilla essence and salt.

2 Melt the butter in a large non-stick frying pan over a medium heat. Meanwhile soak each slice of bread in the egg mixture, turning so it is completely coated. Fry in the butter for about 1 minute each side (until both sides are nice and golden).

3 Drain well on absorbent kitchen paper and keep warm while you fry the rest of the bread. Serve sprinkled with sugar and some strawberries.

This is also great served with sliced banana. If you prefer a savoury version, just season with sea salt and freshly ground black pepper and serve with crispy bacon.

Smoked salmon and scrambled egg breakfast tortilla

Eggs and smoked salmon are a really good combination for breakfast but adding caramelized onions gives this a really different twist – great if you fancy something a little bit different. You can roll the mixture up in soft tortillas or simply serve on top of slightly toasted ones.

PREP TIME 5 minutes
COOKING TIME 25 minutes
SERVES 4

1 tbsp butter
1 tbsp olive oil
2 small onions, thinly sliced
1 tbsp balsamic vinegar
1 tsp brown sugar
salt and freshly ground black
    pepper
125 g (4½ oz) smoked salmon,
    cut into small strips
6 eggs, beaten
1 tbsp grated Parmesan
1 tbsp chives, finely chopped
4 tortillas, warmed

1   First start your onions. Heat the butter and oil in a frying pan over a medium heat, add the onions and cook, stirring, for approximately 10 minutes, until they are soft and golden. Take care not to burn them.

2   Now add the balsamic vinegar and the sugar and cook for a further 10 minutes over a low heat. Add a pinch of salt.

3   Place the salmon pieces into a frying pan over a medium heat and stir until they start to crisp up. Then add the beaten eggs and cook until they just start to set. Stir gently and when the eggs are cooked the way you like them, sprinkle over the Parmesan and chopped chives. Remove from the heat.

4   Warm the tortillas in a pan over a low heat or in the microwave. To serve, divide the egg and salmon mix between the tortillas and top with the caramelized onions. Season to taste and roll or fold as you like.

Lazy Sunday brunch – sausage and portobello bake

My brother gave me this great Sunday brunch recipe for those Sunday mornings when you have a house full of relatives and want to do something a little different to the classic fry-up. It somehow feels a lot easier – maybe it's the simplicity of bringing just one large roasting dish to the table for everyone to just dive in. Now stand back and watch the vultures attack, providing you can bring them plenty of hot buttered toast they should be quiet for at least thirty minutes!

PREP TIME 5 minutes
COOKING TIME approximately 1 hour
SERVES 4 (just double the quantitles for 8)

600 g (1 lb 5 oz) medium new potatoes
olive oil
60 g (2½ oz) cheddar
8 good-quality pork sausages
8 portobello mushrooms
approximately 10 cherry tomatoes on the vine
2–3 thyme sprigs
30 g (1 oz) butter
salt and freshly ground black pepper

1 Preheat the oven to 200°C/400°F/gas 6. Cook the potatoes in a large pan of boiling salted water for about 10 minutes. Drain and tip into a large roasting tray.

2 Drizzle over some olive oil and then bake in the oven for about 45 minutes or until golden. Remove from the oven and leave to cool in the tray. When cool, cut a cross into the top of each potato and fill with a little cheese.

3 Meanwhile, arrange your sausages in a large roasting tray and place in the oven. After 20 minutes turn the sausages and then add the mushrooms, tomatoes and thyme sprigs. Drizzle over some olive oil and add a little sliver of butter to each mushroom. Season with salt and pepper.

4 Return to the oven for a further 20 minutes, adding your pre-roasted potatoes for the final 10 minutes.

5 To serve just let everyone dig in!

Outdoor eating

I have to say I think eating outdoors is one of life's greatest pleasures. It doesn't matter whether it's a beautiful alfresco lunch on a warm summer's day or a trudge over some fields with a flask of soup and some sandwiches – there is something magical about it. Camping is a big thing in our family and I've included some of our favourite 'camp' recipes but you'll also find ideas for barbecues, salads and picnic food. Enjoy!

GO CAMPING!

We really love camping and go every year with a group of parents from our school. One of the highlights for me is definitely the food. Every family mucks in with the cooking and I'm really proud of the fact that we all manage to stay well clear of the classic blackened burger, crispy sausages and crunchy baked beans. Don't get me wrong, there are times when nothing quite fills a gap like burnt sausages. However, this chapter contains some of the recipes for meals we've managed to conjure up with what was brought to camp and I have to say they don't leave me missing the burnt sausages that much!

There are so many different types of campers – from the purists who like to sleep on hard ground and insist on taking as little with them as possible, to the luxury campers who can't do without their feather duvets and cashmere blankets. We probably fall some where in between – I do love my comforts but there's something special about roughing it a little. My kids love the fact that they don't have to have a daily bath and can play football in their pyjamas if they want to. Here are my top camping tips:

- If you are camping in a large group set up a communal area for cooking and eating that all the families can use. If you are trying to travel light, work out beforehand who should bring what, so you are not all bringing the same essentials (first-aid kit, football, cricket bat, games, cards).

- Take turns with the cooking so that each family provides at least one meal.

- Try to arrive at your chosen pitch well before dusk – it's no fun trying to put a tent up in the dark. We usually take one prepared dish with us to have on the first night (see Campfire chilli, page 48).

- Take a small spare tent, if you have one. It can be a great place to keep your clean dry clothes or somewhere to escape to when the rain comes.

- Keep your food stored away carefully at night – hedgehogs, badgers and foxes are used to humans around campsites and can be quite bold!

- Take plenty of foil – it's perfect for cooking over a fire or barbecue.

Potato salad

I love it when new potatoes come into season – they're so delicious plain boiled and served with a little bit of butter but it's nice to do something different with them as well. Charlotte potatoes work really well for this recipe.

PREP TIME 10 minutes
COOKING TIME 20 minutes
SERVES 4–6

1 tbsp cider vinegar
2 tbsp of light mayonnaise
2 tsp Dijon mustard
2 tbsp olive oil
1 tsp honey
salt and freshly
  ground black pepper
1 kg (2 lb 2 oz) new potatoes,
  scrubbed
1 tbsp fresh tarragon
  leaves, chopped
2 tbsp finely chopped
  fresh chives

1 Place the vinegar, mayonnaise, mustard, oil, honey, salt and pepper in a bowl or blender. Whisk or blend well until creamy.

2 Cook the potatoes in boiling salted water for about 15–20 minutes until just tender.

3 Drain well and when cool enough to handle, cut into halves or quarters.

4 Place the potatoes in a mixing bowl with the tarragon and chives, and stir through the dressing, adding as much or as little dressing as you want. This is best done while the potatoes are still slightly warm as they absorb the dressing beautifully.

Potato salad is just fab still slightly warm – although cold is good too!

Homemade coleslaw

This delicious homemade coleslaw can be just as tasty but much lighter simply by trading most of the usual amount of mayonnaise for plain yogurt.

PREP TIME 10 minutes
SERVES 4–6

8 tbsp natural yogurt
½ tsp Dijon mustard
2 tbsp light mayonnaise
½ white cabbage, grated or finely sliced
2 carrots, peeled and grated
½ onion, peeled and finely chopped
juice of ½ lemon
salt and freshly ground black pepper

1 Mix the yogurt, lemon juice, mustard and mayonnaise together in a large bowl.

2 Place all of your prepared vegetables into the bowl and stir through the dressing.

3 Season to taste.

Wholemeal lunchbox pittas

Kids somehow accept wholemeal much easier as a pitta or a wrap rather than bread. These are a great way to cram loads of healthy stuff inside too. The options are endless.

PREP TIME 6 minutes
COOKING TIME 2 minutes
SERVES 2

1 x 185 g (6½ oz) tin tuna
1 tsp olive oil or low-fat
   mayonnaise
small handful alfalfa shoots
handful of salad leaves
   (sweet and crunchy for
   the kids, spinach and
   rocket for the adults
½ cucumber
2 large pitta breads
squeeze of lemon juice
freshly ground black pepper

1 Drain the tuna and mix together with the oil or mayonnaise.

2 Mix the alfalfa shoots in with the salad leaves and slice the cucumber.

3 Place your pittas under a grill to toast. Don't let them get too crispy or they will be hard to fill.

4 Cut each pitta in half and then split open. Add some salad leaves, a few slices of cucumber and a good spoonful of the tuna mixture to each half.

5 Squeeze a little lemon juice over and season with freshly ground black pepper.

Tip
Alfalfa shoots are definitely worth adding to all of your salads, whether in a sandwich or not. They are tasty but, more importantly, about as healthy as healthy can be.

My big fat Greek bruschetta

This is a great camping starter that keeps everyone happy until the main course is ready. It's really easy – and if you don't have a toaster in your camping stove you can just toast the bread in a griddle pan. Serve on a nice big platter and let everyone help themselves.

PREP TIME 5 minutes
COOKING TIME 2 minutes
SERVES 6

For the dressing
2 tbsp olive oil
juice of 1 lemon
150 g (5½ oz) cherry tomatoes, halved
50 g (2 oz) feta cheese, cubed
1 small red onion, chopped
¼ cucumber, finely chopped
50 g (2 oz) black olives, pitted
salt and freshly ground black pepper

For the bruschetta
1 ciabatta loaf
2 tbsp olive oil
salt and freshly ground black pepper

1 To make the dressing mix together the olive oil and lemon juice in a bowl. Add your tomatoes, olives, red onion, cucumber and feta cheese. Season to taste and mix it all together.

2 Split the ciabatta in half and then cut each slice into about three or four pieces and drizzle with a little olive oil. Season and toast the pieces on both sides until golden and crispy.

3 To serve place the toasted bread slices on a big sharing plate and spoon your big fat Greek topping on top.

Tip
The topping can be made any time of the day and covered until the campers are ready.

Sweet chilli chicken kebabs

Tasty, quick and easy for any barbecue or campfire. We like to eat them hot off the barbecue but they are also good cold – you could cook these at home under the grill and take them on a picnic.

PREP TIME 10 minutes,
  plus marinating
COOKING TIME 8–10 minutes
SERVES 4–5

2 skinless and boneless
  chicken breasts
3 tbsp sweet chilli sauce
3 tbsp Chinese oyster sauce

1 If possible, soak the skewers in water for about 30 minutes (this stops them burning on the barbecue or campfire). Mix together the chilli sauce and oyster sauce in a non-metallic bowl.

2 Cut the chicken into bite-sized pieces and add to the bowl, ensuring that all the chicken gets a nice good covering of the marinade. Leave to marinate for at least 20 minutes (longer if possible).

3 Heat the grill or barbecue. While it is heating up, thread the chicken pieces onto the skewers, leaving a little space between each piece. Grill for about 3–5 minutes on each side, or until the chicken is just cooked.

There are so many marinades and sauces that can be used for this. Try experimenting with flavoured oils, herbs, honey and mustard, peanut butter – the list is endless.

Bonnie's jerk-style barbecue chicken

Bonnie is the mother of a good friend of mine, Natalie. Bonnie's parties are a must – especially if you love good party food. This recipe is such a favourite that Bonnie ended up barbecuing 450 pieces of chicken for her son's wedding reception!

PREP TIME 20 minutes, plus marinading
COOKING TIME 40 minutes, approximately
SERVES 6

6 chicken breasts or 12 thighs, skin on
4 tbsp white wine vinegar of juice of a lemon
2 tbsp jerk seasoning from a jar
5 cm (2 in) piece fresh root ginger, peeled and grated
2 tbsp brown sauce
4 tbsp ketchup
2 tbsp vegetable oil
grated rind and juice of 1 lemon
225 g (8 oz) natural yogurt
1 medium onion, peeled and finely chopped
2 garlic cloves, peeled
wood chips for the barbecue, soaked in water for 4–6 hours (try hickory, apple, pear, rosemary or teak)

1 Trim away all the fat from between the chicken breasts or thighs and skin. Leave the skin on. Wash the chicken in cold water mixed with 4 tbsp white vinegar or the juice of a lemon. Drain in a sieve and pat dry with kitchen paper. Place in a large non-metallic bowl.

2 In a food processor, blend all the remaining ingredients (except the wood chips!) to a smooth paste.

3 Using your fingers, tease the marinade into the spaces between the skin and the meat. Cover and refrigerate for 4–6 hours, preferably overnight.

4 Light your coals and wait until they all have a light grey powdery surface. Place a small tin filled with water or apple juice next to the coals. When its contents start to boil, sprinkle the soaked chips over the coals, cover them with foil then place your marinated meat over it.

5 Cover the barbecue to trap the smoke and let the flavour develop. Note which pieces are cooking faster and rotate so that your meat cooks evenly. The slower you cook the meat, the tastier it will be.

Tip

To cook in the oven, just preheat the oven to 180°C/350°F/gas 4. Pop the chicken pieces directly on to the wire runners with a baking tray underneath to catch the drips. Cook for 40–45 minutes.

Even sweeter sweet potato coins

These potatoes are a great addition to any campfire feast or barbecue. If you can't blanch them first don't worry too much – it just stops the surface getting singed before they are cooked through.

PREP TIME 10 minutes
COOKING TIME 10 minutes
SERVES 6

4 small sweet potatoes
110 ml (4 fl oz) olive oil
1 tbsp runny honey
sea salt

1 Bring a large pan of salted water to the boil.

2 Peel and slice the sweet potatoes into 5–10 mm ($\frac{1}{4}$–$\frac{1}{2}$ in) thick slices or 'coins'.

3 Add the sweet potatoes to the boiling water and cook for 2–3 minutes. Drain and immediately plunge into a bowl of iced or cold water.

4 Drain and pat dry with kitchen paper and then place in a large bowl. Mix the oil and honey together and then pour over the sweet potatoes. Toss well to coat.

5 Place sweet potatoes in centre of your barbecue grill rack or griddle. Cook for 4–6 minutes, turning once during cooking time. When they are ready, remove from the grill and sprinkle with sea salt.

Three bean salad

Another great salad which is perfect for a barbecue, summer lunch or picnic.

PREP TIME 10 minutes
COOKING TIME 5 minutes
SERVES 4–6

125 g (4½ oz) green beans
1 x 400 g (14 oz) tin cannellini
   beans
1 x 400 g (14 oz) tin
   black-eyed beans
4 spring onions, finely
   chopped
150 g (5½ oz) mozzarella
   or feta cheese, cut into
   cubes (optional)
4 medium vine-ripened
   tomatoes, sliced
1 tbsp chopped fresh parsley

For the dressing
2 tbsp olive oil
2 tbsp white wine vinegar
1 tbsp of honey
1 tsp mild curry powder
1 garlic clove, peeled and
   crushed
salt and freshly ground
   black pepper

1 First, cook the green beans in a pan of boiling salted water until just tender (about 3–5 minutes). Drain and refresh under cold running water. Drain again and pat dry with kitchen paper. Tip into a large mixing bowl.

2 To make the dressing mix together olive oil, vinegar, honey, curry powder, and the garlic. Stir well and then season to taste.

3 Add the cannellini and black-eyed beans to the green beans, together with the spring onions and mozzarella or feta. Toss together (you can use your hands for this) and then add the dressing.

4 To serve arrange the sliced tomatoes on a large platter and place the dressed beans and mozzarella on top. Finish with some chopped parsley.

Tip
If you are making this for a picnic and aren't too worried about perfect presentation, you can swap the sliced vine tomatoes for cherry tomatoes.

Picnic falafel

A little spin on a Greek meze is a really tasty and healthy alternative to your average picnic fare. These delicious chickpea balls are great as part of a Greek-style picnic and make such a tasty and healthy alternative to boring old sandwiches and crisps. Go the extra mile when packing your picnic and bring plenty of pretty plates, cups, glasses and napkins – and of course a lovely big blanket or two to sit on!

PREP TIME 20 minutes
COOKING TIME 8 minutes
MAKES 16

400 g (14 oz) cooked chickpeas, rinsed and drained
4 tbsp chickpea (gram) flour, plus extra for dusting
½ onion, peeled and chopped
2 tsp coriander seeds, crushed
2 tsp cumin seeds, crushed
3 garlic cloves, peeled and finely chopped
1 green chilli, deseeded and chopped
1 red chilli, deseeded and chopped
1 tbsp fresh coriander, chopped
1 tbsp fresh parsley, chopped
vegetable oil, for frying

1   Place all the ingredients, except the olive oil, in a food processor and blitz until well combined. You are going for a chunky mixture rather than a smooth paste.

2   Using your hands, shape the mixture into small balls about the size of a walnut. Roll each ball in a little chickpea flour.

3   Heat enough oil to just cover the base of a wok or large frying pan until hot. Fry the falafel over a medium heat for about 5–7 minutes, or until golden brown. Cook in batches, transferring the cooked falafel to kitchen paper to drain.

4   When cool these can be packed into an airtight container, ready for your picnic. Serve with hummus, tzatziki, vegetable sticks (we like carrot, red pepper and cucumber batons), olives, cubes of feta cheese and plenty of pitta or flatbread. For something sweet don't forget grapes, strawberries and chunks of watermelon.

Campfire chilli

If you're cooking for a lot of people on a camping trip chillies, soups, casseroles and stews are a great solution – one big pot, and everyone can tuck in. There's nothing better than sitting round the campfire as it gets dark with a bowl of something warm and tasty. You could always do as my friend Jo does and bring a ready-prepared dish. This chilli of hers always goes down really well.

PREP TIME 10 minutes, plus soaking
COOKING TIME 45 minutes
SERVES 6

175 g (6 oz) green lentils
2 tbsp sunflower oil
1 large onion, chopped
1–2 garlic cloves, peeled and crushed
1–2 tsp chilli powder
1 tsp cumin seeds
1 red pepper, deseeded and chopped
1 green pepper, deseeded and chopped
2 carrots, peeled and chopped
2 x 400 g (14 oz) tins chopped tomatoes
1 large tbsp tomato purée

300 ml (½ pint) vegetable stock (use a good-quality stock cube or bouillon powder)
100 g (3½ oz) frozen peas
3 tbsp pesto
175 g (6 oz) mushrooms, wiped and quartered
1 courgette, chopped
salt and freshly ground black pepper
1 x 400 g (14 oz) tin kidney beans, drained and rinsed

To serve
cooked rice
sour cream
grated cheddar
chopped fresh coriander

1 Place the green lentils in a large bowl and pour boiling water over them. Leave to soak for 30 minutes. (Alternatively, buy a tin of pre-soaked lentils.) Drain.

2 Heat the oil in a large saucepan and fry the onion and garlic together with the chilli and cumin seeds, until the onions are softened.

3 Add the peppers, carrots and drained green lentils and cook for 5 minutes, stirring all the time. Add the chopped tomatoes, tomato purée, stock, peas and pesto. Bring to the boil and then simmer until the lentils are tender (about 30 minutes). Add the mushrooms and courgettes and cook for a further 5 minutes. Season to taste.

4 Add the kidney beans and simmer for 5 more minutes.

5 Serve with cooked rice, a dollop of sour cream and grated cheddar, if liked. Sprinkle with a little chopped coriander.

Couscous and spicy sausage salad

Try Spanish chorizo, Polish kabanos or any deli favourite! If you're not keen on spice, look for a milder or plain sausage. Alternatively you could replace the sausage with cubed feta cheese.

PREP TIME 10 minutes
COOKING TIME 10 minutes
SERVES 4

100 g (3½ oz) couscous
200 ml (7 fl oz) hot vegetable
  stock
1 spring onion, sliced
4–6 cherry tomatoes, halved
  or quartered
1 red pepper, deseeded and
  finely chopped
1 yellow pepper, deseeded
  and finely chopped
½ cucumber, chopped
2 tbsp green pesto
2 tbsp pine nuts, toasted
200 g (7 oz) spicy sausage,
  sliced

1 Tip the couscous into a large bowl, and pour over the stock. Cover, and leave for 10 minutes, until nice and fluffy and all the stock has been absorbed.

2 Place the spring onions, tomatoes, red and yellow peppers and cucumber into a large bowl. Fluff up the couscous with a fork and then add to the chopped vegetables. Stir through the pesto and then sprinkle over the pine nuts and the spicy sausage to serve.

Gazpacho

This is such a classic summer dish – I just had to include it. Perfect for lunch in the garden.

PREP TIME 15 minutes
SERVES 4

1 kg (2 lb 2 oz) ripe tomatoes, skinned, deseeded and chopped
1 cucumber, peeled and chopped
2 garlic cloves, peeled and finely chopped
1 small onion, peeled and chopped
1 green pepper, deseeded and chopped
1 red pepper, deseeded and finely chopped
250 ml (9 fl oz) tomato juice
3 tbsp red wine vinegar
3 tbsp olive oil
1 tsp salt
freshly ground black pepper

1 First prepare the tomatoes. Blanch them briefly by placing in a large bowl of boiling water. After a minute you should be able to split the skin and remove it easily. Chop the tomatoes roughly, discarding the seeds.

2 Place the tomatoes, cucumber, garlic, onion and green and red peppers in a blender and process until smooth. If you want a really smooth consistency, pass the mixture through a sieve.

3 Place in a large mixing bowl and add the remaining ingredients, stirring well to combine.

4 Refrigerate for at least 2 hours before serving. Pour into bowls and add one or two ice cubes, a drizzle of olive oil and some freshly ground black pepper. Serve with some crusty bread.

Fruit salad

Let's face it, there isn't much better for your kids than fruit, and a fruit salad is a delicious way to give them some of their 5-a-day. Try this in a lunchbox, on a picnic, for breakfast or even as a between-meals snack.

PREP TIME 10 minutes
SERVES 4–6

For the syrup
1 tbsp caster sugar
125 ml (4 fl oz) cold water
squeeze fresh lime juice or
   1 tbsp lime cordial

150 g (5½ oz) seedless grapes,
2 green apples, cored and
   thickly sliced
2 kiwis, peeled and sliced
natural yogurt, to serve

1   Prepare the syrup by mixing the sugar and water in a bowl until the sugar has dissolved. Add the lime juice or cordial.

2   Prepare your fruit and arrange in a large serving bowl or individual dishes.

3   Pour over the syrup and mix well. Serve immediately with a good dollop of natural yogurt.

Grilled peaches 'n' cream

This is a quick and simple recipe for a really tasty pudding. This is also a good pudding to do on a camping trip or barbecue and definitely one that the kids will love.

PREP TIME 6 minutes
COOKING TIME 5 minutes
SERVES 4

200 g (7 oz) raspberries
200 g (7 oz) blueberries
1 tbsp caster sugar
4 large peaches (nectarines also work well)
3 tbsp runny honey
4 tbsp of fromage frais

1 Place the raspberries and blueberries in a bowl and sprinkle over the caster sugar. Stir gently with a fork to break up the fruit a little.

2 Halve and stone the peaches and place in a shallow dish, cut side up. Drizzle the honey over the peaches and leave until you are ready to cook.

3 Arrange your peaches on the rack, remembering to place them cut side down on the barbecue and cut side up under the grill. Grill under a medium heat for a couple of minutes until they are nice and golden.

4 When they are ready, arrange on a plate and serve with a dollop of fromage frais and the berries scattered over the top. Simple and delicious!

Gooey chocolate bananas

This simple pudding recipe was shared at a barbecue I went to in the summer and I have recreated it a few times on camping trips and at home in the oven. With some simple preparation you will have a really tasty pudding ready in 10 minutes or so.

PREP TIME 5 minutes
COOKING TIME 10–12 minutes
SERVES 4

4 good medium-sized bananas, in their skins
100 g (3½ oz) milk chocolate, chopped
natural yogurt or vanilla ice cream, to serve

1 Preheat the oven to 180°C/350°F/gas 4 or heat the barbecue to a medium heat.

2 Make a cut along the length of the top of the bananas and open slightly. Then press in gently some of the chocolate pieces.

3 Keeping the chocolate side facing upwards wrap the bananas in foil and bake for 10–12 minutes or until the bananas are soft enough and the chocolate has melted.

4 Leave to cool for a few minutes and serve with a dollop of yogurt or vanilla ice cream.

Homemade lemonade

What better way to cool down on a hot summer's day than with a tall glass of this delicious lemonade?

PREP TIME 10 minutes
SERVES 6

8 lemons
175 g (6 oz) granulated sugar
1 litre (1½ pints) cold water
strawberries, halved
fresh mint leaves, to garnish

1 First juice the lemons. You can use a juicer for this or do it by hand, in which case you will need to pass the juice through a sieve to remove the pulp and seeds.

2 Pour the lemon juice and sugar into a large jug and add 1 cup of cold water. Stir well until the sugar has dissolved. Then add the rest of the water.

3 Serve in tall glasses half filled with ice and garnish with strawberry halves and fresh mint sprigs.

Add a small amount of cranberry juice to each glass to transform it into pink lemonade.

Weekend lunches

I love a good roast lunch. It doesn't matter whether I'm cooking for just the five of us or whether we've got a full house of guests, there's something lovely about just popping something in the oven and then pottering round the kitchen preparing vegetables while the kids play outside. Of course there are plenty of other options and this chapter is full of our favourite recipes for relaxed lunching.

Roasted vegetables

This is a great accompaniment to many fish or meat dishes.

PREP TIME 10 minutes
COOKING TIME 35 minutes
SERVES 4–6

450 g (1 lb) new potatoes
1 tbsp chilli oil
1 tbsp chopped garlic
1 large courgette, thickly
　　sliced
1 red pepper, deseeded and
　　cut into chunks
1 yellow pepper, deseeded
　　and cut into chunks
2 red onions, peeled and
　　quartered
2 large tomatoes, quartered
1 tsp dried oregano
salt and freshly ground
　　black pepper

1　Preheat the oven to 190°C/375°F/gas 5. Scrub the potatoes and cook in a large pan of boiling salted water for about 5 minutes. Allow to cool and then cut each one in half.

2　Put the oil and garlic in a large roasting tray and place in the oven for a few minutes to heat up the oil.

3　Add the potatoes and all the other prepared vegetables and toss around to coat in the oil. Add the oregano and seasoning.

4　Cook in the oven for about 30 minutes or until the vegetables are nicely roasted.

Baked Mediterranean tuna

A wonderful way to cook tuna and guests seem to love the novelty of finding a foil wrap on their plates – they can't wait to discover what's inside.

PREP TIME 15 minutes
COOKING TIME 15 minutes
SERVES 4

16 cherry tomatoes, halved
1 large garlic clove, peeled
   and finely chopped
1 red onion, peeled and
   finely chopped
handful of fresh basil,
   chopped
juice of 1 lemon
4 tbsp olive oil, plus extra
   for drizzling
salt and freshly ground black
   pepper
4 fresh tuna steaks, about
   175 g (6 oz) each
250 ml (9 fl oz) dry white
   wine

1 Preheat the oven to 220°C/425°F/gas 7.

2 Place the tomatoes, garlic, onion, basil, lemon juice and oil in a bowl and mix well, seasoning to taste. Set aside for about 10 minutes so the flavours can infuse.

3 Prepare the fish by drizzling with a little olive oil and rubbing in with your hands. Season with salt and pepper. Now take four pieces of foil approximately 40–50 cm (16–20 in) long, fold in half then open out again. Divide the tomato and onion mixture between the four pieces of foil and then place a tuna steak on top of each one. Fold up the sides of the foil to make a loose parcel, adding a splash of white wine before you seal each one.

4 Place the foil parcels on a baking tray or ovenproof dish and place in the oven. Cook for about 10–12 minutes and then remove from the oven. Leave the fish to stand for a further 5 minutes before opening. Serve with new potatoes and some fresh green vegetables.

Tuna with aromatic rice

Tuna is such a versatile fish; it can be cooked on a griddle pan just like a steak, baked in foil, casseroled in chunks or barbecued to perfection. The list is endless and I think we have tried all of the above with great success. Another reason why we love it so much is that it, if cooked well, it is a great fish to start children on – especially if your little ones are put off by the 'fishy' smell that a lot of fish have. As an oily fish, it's also a great source of Omega 3.

PREP TIME 10 minutes,
    plus marinating
COOKING TIME 15 minutes
SERVES 4

2 tbsp olive oil
120 ml (4 fl oz) fresh orange
    juice
5 cm (2 in) piece fresh root
    ginger, peeled and finely
    grated
salt and freshly ground black
    pepper
4 fresh tuna steaks, about
    175 g (6 oz) each
250 g (9 oz) basmati rice
300 g (10 oz) tenderstem
    broccoli
1 tsp grated orange zest
handful chopped coriander

1   First make the marinade. Place the olive oil, orange juice, grated ginger and black pepper in a shallow, non-metallic dish and stir well. Add the tuna steaks and turn to coat in the marinade. Cover and leave in the refrigerator for at least 2 hours.

2   Rinse the basmati rice under plenty of cold running water and cook according to the packet instructions. Meanwhile, bring a separate pan of salted water to the boil for the broccoli.

3   Place a non-stick frying pan or griddle over a high heat. Remove the tuna steaks from the marinade and cook for 2 minutes on each side, adding a little of the marinade to the pan. Add the broccoli to the boiling water and cook for just a couple of minutes (it should still retain some 'bite').

4   Remove the tuna from the pan, cover and keep warm. Drain the rice and stir through the orange zest, chopped coriander and some black pepper. Serve with the drained broccoli and tuna steaks.

Ibiza Town pasta dish

We had this dish (or something very like it) in a little bar in Ibiza years ago.
I've recreated it at home several times since, although it's probably not quite
the same as the original. We love this version.

PREP TIME 10 minutes
COOKING TIME 20 minutes
SERVES 4

300 g (10½ oz) fusilli pasta
1 small head of broccoli, cut
    into small florets
1 tbsp olive oil
1 small garlic clove, peeled
    and finely chopped
100 ml (3½ fl oz) white wine
285 ml (10 fl oz) single cream
125 g (4½ oz) smoked salmon,
    cut into strips
freshly ground black pepper
fresh basil, to garnish

1 Cook the pasta in boiling salted water according to the
packet instructions. A few minutes before the end of
the cooking time, add the broccoli florets.

2 Meanwhile heat the oil in a large pan and add the garlic
and herbs. Cook for a couple of minutes, taking care
not to brown the garlic. Pour in the white wine and
bring to the boil.

3 Remove from the heat and stir in the cream. Return to
a low heat and simmer for a couple of minutes until the
sauce starts to thicken. Add the smoked salmon pieces
and stir through – the salmon will turn pale pink.

4 Finally add the drained pasta and broccoli and gently
mix together. Season with freshly ground black pepper
and top with a few fresh basil leaves. Serve with lots
of crusty bread.

Gorgeous fish pie

This is a gorgeous fish pie for the all the family as it's not too creamy and rich. You can vary it by using different fish, although I like to use a mixture of smoked and unsmoked fish. A handful of prawns also works well.

PREP TIME 30 minutes
COOKING TIME 45 minutes
SERVES 4–6

600 ml (20 fl oz) semi-
    skimmed milk
1 onion, peeled and sliced
few black peppercorns
1 bay leaf
300 g (10 oz) skinless smoked
    haddock fillet
300 g (10 oz) skinless
    white fish (such as cod)
200 g (7 oz) skinless
    salmon fillet
50 g (2 oz) butter
50 g (2 oz) plain flour
1 tbsp chopped fresh parsley
salt and freshly ground
    black pepper
1 kg (2 lb 2 oz) floury potatoes,
    peeled
30 g (1 oz) butter, melted

1 First poach your fish. Pour the milk into a large pan (big enough to hold all the fish) and add the sliced onion, peppercorns and bay leaf. Add the fish to the milk and bring slowly to the boil. Reduce to a low simmer and leave for about 6 minutes. Lift the fish from the pan, set the milk aside for now.

2 When cool enough to handle, flake the fish into a large ovenproof dish. Strain the milk into a jug.

3 To make the sauce, melt the butter in a pan and stir in the flour. Reduce the heat and add some of the poaching milk. Stir quickly as the sauce thickens and then gradually add the rest of the milk, stirring and blending as you go. Add the chopped parsley and season to taste. Pour the sauce over the fish and set aside while you prepare the potatoes.

4 Preheat the oven to 190°C/375°F/gas 5. Bring a large pan of boiling salted water to the boil and parboil the potatoes for about 5–8 minutes. Drain thoroughly and set aside. When cool enough to handle cut the potatoes into thick slices. Arrange these in a single layer on top of your fish, overlapping each slice as you go. Brush the top with melted butter and bake in the oven for 25–30 minutes, or until the topping is golden brown.

Tip

You can, of course, go down the more traditional route and mash the potatoes. Using half potatoes and half sweet potatoes also works well. Some people like to sprinkle over grated cheddar before popping in the oven.

Cod roasted in lemon and thyme

A lot of children find fish difficult – maybe it's something about the texture and smell. Cod is one of the few varieties that seems to get the thumbs up. I also find roasting or grilling are much better ways of cooking the fish without it releasing whatever it is that only kids under 10 can smell!

PREP TIME 5 minutes
COOKING TIME 15 minutes
SERVES 4

4 fresh cod loin fillets,
   about 175 g (6 oz) each
2–3 tbsp of olive oil
75 g (2½ oz) fresh
   breadcrumbs
2 lemons
pinch of dried oregano
5 sprigs of thyme, leaves
   picked off one
salt and freshly ground
   black pepper

1 Preheat the oven to 220°C/425°F/gas 7. Use your hands to rub the olive oil over the cod fillets.

2 Grate the rind of one of the lemons and mix together with the breadcrumbs and herbs and then loosely press this mixture on top of each piece of fish. Season with salt and freshly ground black pepper.

3 Place the cod in a roasting tray, drizzle with a little more olive oil and add in the remaining sprigs of thyme and lemons, cut into quarters.

4 Cook in the top part of the oven for 10–12 minutes. Serve with lemon wedges, new potatoes and a fresh green salad.

The ultimate spaghetti bolognese

This is such an old favourite and if you've never given it a go, it's a must. I know there are hundreds of versions of this dish out there and plenty of purists who insist it should be done one way or another, but this is how I like to cook it. I usually make a big batch of this – somehow it always seems to taste better the next day! This is one of Wayne's favourites.

PREP TIME 20 minutes
COOKING TIME 2 hours
SERVES 6–8

2 tbsp olive oil
500 g (1 lb 2 oz) lean beef mince
1 large onion, chopped
3 garlic cloves, peeled and finely chopped
2 sticks celery, finely chopped
1 carrot, finely chopped
75 g (2½ oz) mushrooms, sliced
250 ml (9 fl oz) red wine
2 tbsp tomato purée
400 ml (14 fl oz) beef stock
1 x 400 g (14 oz) tin chopped tomatoes
1 tbsp Worcestershire sauce
2 tbsp fresh oregano, chopped
400 g (14 oz) dried spaghetti

To serve
fresh basil leaves
grated Parmesan

1 Heat 2 tbsp of the oil in a large pan and add the beef mince – you want the meat to get nicely sealed and browned (you can do this in batches if you want). Remove from the pan with a slotted spoon and set aside.

2 Now add the onion and garlic, adding a little more oil if necessary. Cook gently for about 5 minutes and then add the celery, carrot and mushrooms and cook for a further 5 minutes.

3 Add the red wine and cook for a couple of minutes, scraping any residue off the bottom of the pan. Return the mince to the pan and add the tomato purée, beef stock, tinned tomatoes, Worcestershire sauce and oregano.

4 Bring to the boil, stirring, and then reduce the heat to a low simmer. Cover and leave to cook for about 1½ hours. Remember to check on it from time to time to make sure it is not drying out.

5 When you are nearly ready to eat, cook the spaghetti according to the packet instructions. Serve the bolognese with some fresh basil leaves and plenty of grated Parmesan.

Tip
There are so many ways you can adapt this dish – try adding different vegetables, such as red pepper, courgette or finely chopped leeks. You could also try lamb mince or quorn mince, which is a tasty and healthy alternative.

Yorkshire cheesy-topped cottage pie

I find this is a great dish when you have friends round for a casual weekend lunch – you can prepare it in advance (even the day before) and just pop in the oven when you're ready.

PREP TIME 20 minutes
COOKING TIME 1½ hours
SERVES 6

2 tbsp oil
900 g (2 lb) lean minced beef
1 large onion, chopped
1 large carrot chopped
2 tbsp plain flour
½ tsp ground cinnamon
2 tbsp tomato purée
1 tsp dried thyme
600 ml (1 pint) beef stock
salt and freshly ground
    black pepper
2 tbsp chopped fresh parsley

For the topping
700 g (1½ lb) old potatoes,
    peeled and cut into chunks
450 g (1 lb) parsnips, cut into
    chunks
4 tbsp mayonnaise
75 g (2½ oz) mature cheddar,
    grated
30 g (1 oz) butter, melted

1   Heat 1 tbsp oil in a large heavy-based pan and brown the mince over a high heat, stirring. Lift out and set aside.

2   Heat the remaining oil in the pan and fry the onion and carrot over a medium heat for 5 minutes until soft.

3   Return the meat to the pan, add the flour, cinnamon and tomato purée, and cook for 1 minute. Stir in the thyme stock and salt and pepper. Bring to the boil, cover and simmer gently for 35–40 minutes. Skim off the fat, add the parsley and check the seasoning.

4   Preheat the oven to 200°C/400°F/gas 6. Bring a large pan of salted water to the boil and add the potatoes and parsnips. Cook for about 20 minutes until soft. Drain and return to the pan and then mash. Stir in the mayonnaise and cheese.

5   Spoon the meat into a deep ovenproof dish. Pile the mash on top and use a fork to push to the edges. Brush with the melted butter and cook in the oven for 25 minutes or until golden on top.

Gratin of potato and mushrooms

This is a wonderful side dish but it also works well as a main dish with a nice big side salad and some crusty bread.

PREP TIME 20 minutes
COOKING TIME 1 hour
SERVES 6

250 g (9 oz) large field
   mushrooms
800 g (1 lb 12 oz) floury
   potatoes
30 g (1 oz) butter
1 garlic clove, peeled and
   finely chopped
300 ml (10 fl oz) single cream
4 tbsp grated Parmesan
salt and freshly ground
   black pepper

1 Preheat the oven to 180°C/350°F/gas 4.

2 Wipe clean the mushrooms and slice thinly – you could also try adding a few wild mushrooms such as chanterelle. Peel the potatoes and slice thinly.

3 Bring a large pan of salted water to the boil and add the potato slices. As soon as the water returns to the boil, drain thoroughly and leave to cool. Spread the slices out on some kitchen paper.

4 Grease an ovenproof dish with the butter and sprinkle over the garlic. Arrange about half the sliced potatoes in a layer in the dish and then add a layer of mushrooms. Top with the remaining potatoes (it looks nice if you overlap the potatoes to create a scallop effect).

5 Place the cream in a pan and bring gently to the boil, then pour over the potatoes. Scatter the Parmesan on top and bake in the oven for 1 hour until it is crisp and golden and the cream is bubbling.

Spicy potatoes

This is a family recipe that my Mum and Granny both used to cook – it's a great way to spice up potatoes.

PREP TIME 20 minutes
COOKING TIME 20 minutes
SERVES 6–8

900 g (2 lb) potatoes
30 g (1 oz) butter
1 medium onion, peeled and
    sliced
1 tbsp curry powder
1 tbsp flour
300 ml (10 fl oz) milk
salt and freshly ground
    black pepper
55 g (2 oz) grated cheddar

1 Scrub the potatoes but do not peel them. Bring a large pan of salted water to the boil and cook the potatoes until just tender. Drain.

2 When they are cool enough to handle, cut the potatoes into thick slices and put them in a lightly greased ovenproof dish.

3 To make the sauce melt the butter in pan over a medium heat. Add the onion and cook gently for about 5 minutes until the onions are softened. Add the curry powder and cook for another couple of minutes before adding the flour. Stir through the onions.

4 Add the milk and stir over a gentle heat until it comes to the boil. Let it simmer for 1–2 minutes and then season to taste.

5 Pour the sauce over the potatoes and top with the grated cheese. Place under a hot grill until the top is golden and bubbling. Serve immediately.

Go easy on the curry powder at first if your children aren't used to spices.

Brocky's Jubilee chicken

This is a recipe for a great family dish, given to us by Melinda's uncle – his surname is Brock, hence the name. It's really colourful and tomatoey.

PREP TIME 10 minutes
COOKING TIME 40 minutes
SERVES 4

8–10 spring onions
2 tbsp olive oil
4 skinless chicken breasts
2 tbsp tomato purée
3 tsp sweet chilli bean sauce
2 x 400 g (14 oz) tins chopped
   tomatoes
2 peppers (yellow or red),
   deseeded and sliced
300 g (10 oz) mushrooms,
   quartered

1 Finely chop the spring onions, including as much green stalk as is useable. Heat the oil in a large frying pan or wok add cook the spring onions for 1–2 minutes.

2 Add the chicken breasts to the pan and seal on all sides – this should take about 5 minutes. Add the tomato purée, chilli bean sauce and chopped tomatoes. Bring to the boil and add the peppers and mushrooms.

3 Cover and reduce the heat. Leave to simmer for about 30 minutes, checking occasionally. Serve with plain rice.

Chinese chicken rice

This is a really easy dish – everything you need in one bowl! You can vary the ingredients – turkey or quorn pieces also work well.

PREP TIME 20 minutes
COOKING TIME 20 minutes
SERVES 6

1 tbsp vegetable oil
1 onion, peeled and chopped
4 rashers bacon, chopped
2 garlic cloves, peeled and
    crushed
handful of mushrooms, sliced
1 carrot, chopped
500 g (1 lb 2 oz) rice
1½ tsp turmeric
1 tbsp mixed herbs
500 ml (1 pint) chicken stock
400 g (14 oz) mixed
    vegetables (peas, baby corn,
    sliced mangetout)
3 cooked chicken breasts
handful of cooked prawns
    (optional)
1 tbsp soy sauce
salt and freshly ground
    black pepper

1 Heat the oil in a wok or large frying pan and add the onion and bacon. Cook for about 5 minutes and then add the garlic, mushrooms and carrot.

2 Add the dry rice to wok, along with the turmeric and herbs. Stir so that each grain of rice is coated in the oil.

3 Add about half the stock, bring to the boil and then reduce the heat. Leave to simmer for about 8 minutes, stirring occasionally and adding more stock as you go. Add the vegetables and continue to cook for about 2–3 minutes until the rice is cooked and has absorbed the liquid.

4 Add the cooked chicken and prawns (if using) and continue cooking until warmed through. Add the soy sauce and season to taste.

Roasted chicken with garlic butter and thyme

Friends coming for Sunday lunch? I have the perfect tip for the best roast chicken. It may seem a bit fiddly and messy but the results are well worth it. The chicken is tasty, aromatic and moist beyond belief.

PREP TIME 15 minutes
COOKING TIME 1–1½ hours
SERVES 4–5

1 medium free-range chicken
100 g (3½ oz) softened butter
3 thyme sprigs, leaves picked
    and chopped
2 garlic cloves, peeled and
    finely chopped
salt and freshly ground
    black pepper

1 Preheat the oven to 220°C/425°F/gas 7. Remove the giblets, if any, from the chicken and then weigh the bird to calculate the cooking time.

2 Mix the garlic and thyme together with the butter until smooth in texture. Add seasoning to taste.

3 You now have to try and get under the skin of the chicken and spread it with the garlic butter. Be gentle as you do not want to rip the skin. You can do this with a piping bag but Wayne prefers to use his hands! It can usually be done with a small slit at the bottom of each breast, don't worry if the skin does split, it just contains the juices better if it's not. You are looking to achieve a fairly equal covering across the whole of the chicken.

4 Secure the neck end of the chicken with a few cocktail sticks and then place in a roasting tin. Cook in the oven for 30 minutes and then reduce the temperature to 160°C/325°F/gas 3. Continue to cook for a further 15–30 minutes for a 1–1.5 kg (2–3 lb) bird and 30–60 minutes for a 1.5–2.5 kg (3–5 lb) bird. Check the bird every 10 minutes or so and use a spoon to baste with the juice.

5 To test if the chicken is done insert a skewer into the thickest part of the thigh. If the juices run clear the chicken is cooked. Remove from the oven and leave to rest for 15–20 minutes before carving. Use the pan juices to make your gravy.

Minted lamb chops

This is a delicious way to enjoy your lamb chops. The method is quite similar to the plaice goujons (see page 100), but with some freshly chopped mint thrown in, which really complements the lamb.

PREP TIME 10 minutes
COOKING TIME 15 minutes
SERVES 2

100 g (3½ oz) fresh
  breadcrumbs
2 tbsp fresh mint,
  finely chopped
1 tbsp fresh parsley,
  finely chopped
salt and freshly ground
  black pepper
flour, for coating
1 egg, beaten
4 lamb chops
1 tbsp olive oil

1 Place the breadcrumbs, mint and parsley in a bowl and mix until evenly combined. Alternatively you can whizz them together in a food processor. Add salt and pepper to taste.

2 Place the flour in one shallow dish and the beaten egg in another. Coat each chop in the flour, then dip in the egg and finally press into the breadcrumbs until nicely coated.

3 Heat the oil in a frying pan over a medium heat. Add the lamb chops and cook until nicely browned on each side. Try not to move them around in the pan too much as you don't want the coating to crumble off.

4 If your chops and quite small and you like them slightly pink you can continue to cook them for a few more minutes in the pan. Alternatively transfer the chops to a baking tray and finish them off in a preheated oven (180°C/350°F/gas 4) for about 10 minutes.

5 Serve the chops with some minted new potatoes and a beetroot and carrot salad.

Teatime treats and simple suppers

Those few hours after school are often the trickiest time of the day – the kids are ravenous so you need to be able to conjure up something fast. Some of these are quick bites you can rustle up in no time, some of them are ideal if you prepare in advance. Whether it's a quick carbonara or a pizza muffin, there are plenty of recipes in this chapter to keep you inspired.

STORECUPBOARD ESSENTIALS

We all know that we should be shopping locally for food but for most of us the reality is often a massive weekly shop at the supermarket. Try to buy your meat, fish and vegetables as and when you need them but stock up on these essentials. With a well stocked cupboard, freezer and fridge and a bit of organization it's always possible to rustle up something tasty for the kids.

Freezer

- frozen peas

- breadcrumbs – don't throw out slightly stale slices of bread – just whizz them into breadcrumbs in your food processor and then keep in the freezer. They hardly need any defrosting and are great for making goujons and burgers.

- bagels and pitta breads – just pop straight into the toaster.

- frozen berries – if you crave fruity smoothies in the middle of winter this is a great option and much better than buying fresh berries out of season.

- packets of smoked salmon will defrost in no time.

- frozen prawns – unless you are buying raw prawns for a special dish there is nothing wrong with using cooked frozen prawns – and they defrost quickly.

- ice cream – need I say more?

Fridge

- cheese – hard cheeses like Parmesan and cheddar will keep for a long time if wrapped properly.

- fresh herbs – chives, parsley and coriander will keep for much longer in the fridge if wrapped in damp kitchen paper and popped into a plastic bag. If you can grow your own herbs in pots on the kitchen windowsill, even better!

- crème fraîche – great for pasta sauces (I prefer the half-fat version).

- eggs – for omelettes, pancakes, cakes – you name it.

Cupboard

- dried pasta in a variety of shapes

- rice (white and brown)

- dried noodles

- pine nuts – great for adding to pasta dishes and, of course, making your own pesto.

- couscous

- porridge oats

- pulses – dried or tinned

- tinned tuna – perfect for sandwiches, salads and jacket potatoes.

- baked beans – every cupboard should have this standby!

- stock cubes – look out for good-quality or organic brands.

- superfoods – we always have brazil nuts, cashews, sunflower, pumpkin and poppy seeds, dried cranberries and goji berries – great for snacking or cooking.

- cake decorations – you never know when the urge for fairy cakes will take you!

- meringue nests – perfect for mini pavlovas (see page 132).

- chocolate – for melting and cooking – not eating!

Pizza muffins

This is a fun way for kids to try their hand at mini pizzas. You could go all out and make your own pizza bases but crumpets and muffins make a great alternative and are really quick to prepare.

PREP TIME 10 minutes
COOKING TIME 5 minutes
SERVES 6

400 g (14 oz) tin chopped
   tomatoes, drained
1 tsp mixed herbs
1 garlic clove, peeled and
   crushed
salt and freshly ground
   black pepper
6 English muffins or
   crumpets
200 g (7 oz) mozzarella, sliced
fresh basil leaves

1 Place the tomatoes, herbs and garlic into a bowl. Mix and season to taste.

2 Split the muffins and then place under a hot grill, lightly toasting on one side. Spoon over the tomato mix, then add the mozzarella slices. Return to the grill and cook for 1–2 minutes until the cheese has melted.

3 Top with a sprinkle of pepper and a couple of torn leaves of basil.

Tip
You could try adding some strips of ham or halved cherry tomatoes

Spelt pasta with king prawns

When you have very little time to cook you often end up hitting the beans on toast or the curry house at the end of the road – no need! This dish takes 10 minutes and that includes cooking the pasta. Our cupboards and fridge are almost always stocked with the majority of these ingredients so the option of rustling up something like this is always at hand.

PREP TIME 10 minutes
COOKING TIME 10 minutes
SERVES 4

400 g (14 oz) spelt spaghetti
4 tbsp olive oil
juice of 1 lemon
juice of ½ lime
150 g (5½ oz) Parmesan,
  freshly grated
handful of fresh basil leaves,
  roughly torn
1 tbsp pine nuts, toasted
250 g (9 oz) king prawns
8 cherry tomatoes, halved
freshly ground black pepper

1 Cook the pasta according to the packet instructions.

2 Meanwhile put 3 tablespoons of olive oil, the lemon and lime juices in a bowl and mix together. Now stir in the Parmesan, basil leaves and toasted pine nuts. Add pepper to taste.

3 Heat the remaining olive oil in a wok or large frying pan and add the prawns and cherry tomatoes. Gently fry for about 2–3 minutes. Remove from the heat and leave to cool a little. Then add to the olive oil, Parmesan, basil and pine nut mixture.

4 Drain the pasta thoroughly and add to the prawn mixture. Heat gently as you stir through, making sure the spaghetti is well covered. Serve immediately.

Tip

This dish can work with so many different ingredients. Try ready-cooked smoked salmon flakes, gently fried quorn (chicken-style) pieces, tofu or even chicken.

Pasta with simple tomato sauce

This is a real no-brainer. Most kids love pasta and tomatoes are a great source of vitamins so this ticks all the boxes.

PREP TIME 15 minutes
COOKING TIME 30 minutes
SERVES 4

680 g (1½ lb) ripe tomatoes
1 tbsp olive oil
1 garlic clove, peeled and
   finely chopped
generous pinch of mixed
   herbs
salt and freshly ground black
   pepper
400 g (14 oz) dried pasta
8 basil leaves, torn into
   small pieces

1 Cut a small cross in the bottom of each tomato and place them in a heatproof bowl of boiling water. Leave for a couple of minutes while you fill up a second bowl with cold water.

2 Using a large spoon transfer the tomatoes from the hot water into the cold and leave them for another 2 minutes.

3 Remove the tomatoes and carefully peel off the skins. Cut each one into quarters and remove the cores and seeds (if you prefer a seedless sauce). Chop the tomatoes into dice and set aside, keeping as much of the juice as possible.

4 Heat 1 tablespoon of olive oil in a large pan and add the garlic, tomatoes, herbs and seasoning to taste. Heat over a medium heat for a couple of minutes then cover and turn down the heat. Leave for about 15–20 minutes, stirring occasionally. If the tomatoes look they are drying out, add a splash of water.

5 Meanwhile cook the pasta in a large pan of boiling salted water, or according to the packet instructions. Drain well and divide among 4 pasta bowls.

6 Stir the basil leaves into your tomato sauce and serve on top of the pasta. Top with a few extra basil leaves to garnish.

Howard's rice meal

Howard is a very good friend of the family and his rice meal is full of goodness, quick to prepare, and very tasty. The wild and long grain rice is healthy, unprocessed and adds variety and colour to your dish, along with the variety of vegetables.

PREP TIME 20 minutes
COOKING TIME 20 minutes
SERVES 4

150 g (5 oz) long-grain rice
50 g (2 oz) wild rice
1 tbsp vegetable bouillon powder
75 g (3 oz) frozen peas, defrosted
100 g (4 oz) broccoli
2 tbsp olive oil
2 garlic cloves, peeled and crushed
2 cm (½ in) fresh root ginger,
    peeled and finely chopped
2 red onions, peeled and chopped
1 red pepper, deseeded and
    chopped
150 g (5 oz) button mushrooms,
    quartered
1 x 400 g (14 oz) tin chopped
    tomatoes
150 g (5 oz) cherry tomatoes
pinch of dried oregano
pinch of dried thyme
1 tsp soy sauce

1 Cook the rice according to the packet instructions, adding the vegetable bouillon powder to the boiling water. You may need to do this in two separate pans as cooking times can vary.

2 Five minutes before the rice is ready, add the peas and broccoli to one of the pans. Do not cook for longer than 5 minutes – you want the vegetables to have some bite.

3 Heat the oil in a wok or large frying pan and add the garlic, ginger, onions and red pepper. Cook for 1–2 minutes, stirring, and then add the mushrooms, cherry tomatoes and dried herbs. Cook for a further 2 minutes and then add the chopped tomatoes and soy sauce. Heat through for a couple more minutes and then cover and turn down the heat until you are ready to add the rice.

4 Drain the rice, peas and broccoli thoroughly and then add to the wok or frying pan. Increase the heat while you stir the rice through the vegetables. Serve immediately.

There you have it: a quick, healthy, colourful and tasty dish which can easily be altered to suit your (and your children's) tastes.

Mushroom omelette

Omelettes are simple, easy and a great way of rustling up a delicious supper for the children. You can vary the filling depending on whatever you have lying around in the fridge that day. Mushrooms are my favourite and luckily my children like them too – here is my recipe for four people. Two eggs per person is about right.

PREP TIME 15 minutes
COOKING TIME 5 minutes
SERVES 4

450 g (1 lb) button
   mushrooms, sliced
2 tbsp butter, plus extra
   for frying
8 eggs
2 tbsp crème fraîche
handful chives, finely
   chopped
salt and freshly ground
   black pepper

1 Cut the mushrooms into thick slices, and gently fry in 2 tablespoons of the butter in a frying pan.

2 Now whisk the eggs by hand for about 5 minutes until they are nice and frothy. Whisk in the crème fraîche and chives, leaving a few for the garnish. Season to taste.

3 In a separate frying pan melt the remaining butter on a low heat and pour in about a quarter of the egg mixture. Cook for about 2 minutes.

4 When the omelette is done around the edges but still soft and runny in the middle, add a quarter of the mushrooms and cook for a further minute or two until it is set but still soft.

5 Place the omelette onto a plate and fold it in half. Garnish with finely chopped chives and then repeat to make the rest of the omelettes.

Quorn coconut curry

We eat a lot of quorn at home – it's an excellent source of protein and is very low in fat. Cutting down on the amount of meat we all eat is beneficial on so many levels so this is a good alternative. Quorn takes many forms including quorn mince and 'chicken-style' pieces, which is what I have used here.

PREP TIME 10 minutes
COOKING TIME 40 minutes
SERVES 4

2 tsp cornflour
250 ml (9 fl oz) natural
  yogurt
2 tbsp olive oil
1 onion, peeled and finely
  chopped
2 garlic cloves, peeled and
  finely chopped
½ tsp ground turmeric
2 tsp ground coriander
1 tsp ground cumin
300 g (10 oz) quorn pieces
300 ml (10 fl oz) coconut milk
1 vegetable stock cube mixed
  with 75 ml (2½ fl oz)
  boiling water
salt and freshly ground
  black pepper
2 tbsp chopped fresh
  coriander

1   Mix the cornflour and yogurt in a bowl, adding a couple of tablespoons of yogurt at a time.

2   Heat the oil in a wok or large pan and add the onion. Cook slowly for about 10 minutes until the onions are soft and golden brown. Add the garlic, turmeric, coriander and cumin cook for a further 2 minutes, stirring well.

3   Reduce the heat and add the quorn pieces to the pan. Then stir in the yogurt mixture, a tablespoon at a time.

4   Add the coconut milk and vegetable stock paste, stirring slowly. Season to taste. Cover and leave for 25 minutes, stirring occasionally. Garnish with fresh coriander and serve with basmati rice and naan bread.

Grilled chicken with roasted vegetables

Delicious and healthy.

PREP TIME 15 minutes
COOKING TIME 30 minutes
SERVES 4

2 large leeks, cut into chunks
1 red pepper, deseeded and
    sliced
1 large red onion, peeled
    and sliced
150 ml (5 fl oz) vegetable stock
4 skinless and boneless
    chicken breasts
olive oil, for brushing
juice of ½ lime
1 tbsp pine nuts, toasted
salt and freshly ground
    black pepper

1 Preheat the oven to 200°C/400°F/gas 6.

2 Put the leeks, pepper and onion in a roasting tin and pour over the vegetable stock. Season well with salt and pepper and roast for approximately 30 minutes stirring through occasionally. (We like the vegetables crunchy, you may need to increase the time.)

3 Meanwhile place the chicken on a grill pan and brush with a little olive oil, squeeze over the lime juice and season well. Grill for 8–10 minutes on each side until cooked.

4 When the vegetables are ready divide between four plates and sprinkle over the pine nuts. Top each plate with a piece of grilled chicken and spoon over the juices from the roasting tin.

5 Serve immediately with a rocket and spinach salad.

Homemade burgers

Kids love burgers and there's no reason why they can't be a healthy option. Just serve with plenty of salad in a wholemeal bun and have some homemade potato wedges on the side (see page 103). Kids love helping too, just make sure their hands are clean!

PREP TIME 10 minutes
COOKING TIME 20 minutes
MAKES 4–6 burgers

1 tbsp olive oil
1 shallot, very finely chopped
500 g (1 lb 2 oz) lean beef
    mince
1 tsp garlic salt
1 egg, beaten
freshly ground black pepper

To serve
lettuce leaves
cucumber, tomato and onion
    slices
sliced cheddar cheese
wholemeal or granary rolls

1 Heat the oil in a pan and add the chopped shallot. Cook over a low heat for about 5 minutes until softened (you do not want the shallot to colour that much).

2 Place the mince, shallot, garlic salt and beaten egg and pepper in a large bowl and mix together. You may need to use your hands to mix it thoroughly.

3 Divide the mixture equally and use your hands to form the mixture into balls (you may want to make 4 medium sized burgers or 6 smaller ones). Flatten each one into a burger shape.

4 Place them under a medium to hot grill and cook for 10–12 minutes turning frequently – make sure they are cooked through before serving.

There are so many variations to this basic recipe – you can add whatever flavourings you like. Just make sure that any extra ingredients are finally chopped. Try from the following:

- sweet chilli sauce
- mixed herbs
- fresh parsley
- garlic
- mushrooms
- spring onions

Pasta carbonara

When it's pasta in the evenings for the kids it's usually a simple decision between bolognese and carbonara – for them it's either 'the creamy one' or 'the red one'. This version is so much healthier than the ready-made sauces you find on supermarket shelves – most of which are full of salt and sugar. It's also great if you use wholemeal pasta. Make it more interesting by varying the pasta shapes – I was amazed when I started looking just how may different kinds of pasta were available these days.

PREP TIME 5 minutes
COOKING TIME 15 minutes
SERVES 4

300 g (10 oz) wholemeal pasta
4 eggs
150 ml (5 fl oz) single cream
    (you could also use crème
    fraîche)
40 g (1½ oz) cheddar, grated
1 tbsp chopped fresh parsley
salt and freshly ground
    black pepper
60 g (2½ oz) cooked ham,
    sliced into strips

1 Cook your pasta according to the packet instructions.

2 Meanwhile place the eggs in a mixing bowl and whisk together, then slowly add in the cream, half the cheese, half the parsley and a little salt and pepper. Make sure everything is whisked thoroughly together.

3 When your pasta is cooked drain it and return it to the pan. Then slowly mix in the cream and egg mixture, adding the ham little by little to ensure it is evenly combined.

4 Serve immediately sprinkled with the remaining cheese and parsley.

Plaice goujons

Who needs fish fingers when you can make your own? This is also a really fun way of getting the children involved in the kitchen as they really enjoy the assembly line required for the coating.

PREP TIME 20 minutes
COOKING TIME 10 minutes
SERVES 4

500 g (1 lb) skinless and
  boneless plaice fillet
2 tbsp self-raising flour
2 eggs, beaten
100 g (3½ oz) fresh
  breadcrumbs
salt and freshly ground
  black pepper to taste
lemon wedges, to serve

For the tartare sauce
2 tbsp mayonnaise
1 tbsp baby capers, chopped
1 tbsp gherkins, finely
  chopped
1 tbsp chopped fresh
  flat-leaf parsley
juice of ½ lemon
salt and freshly ground
  black pepper

1 First make the tartare sauce. Place the mayonnaise, capers, gherkins and parsley in a bowl and mix well. Add a squeeze of lemon juice and season to taste.

2 Cut your plaice into goujons, sliced at a 45-degree angle.

3 Set up your assembly line by putting the flour, beaten egg and breadcrumbs in three separate plates or shallow dishes. Add salt and pepper to the flour. Have a child at each station!

4 Dip each goujon into the flour, then the egg and then the breadcrumbs. Take care not to drown the goujons in egg. As each one is ready, place on a tray or chopping board ready for cooking.

5 If you are using a deep-fat fryer, set the temperature to 190°C/375°F. Alternatively heat the oil in a large heavy-based pan. It is hot enough when a cube of bread turns golden brown in about 30 seconds. Fry the goujons in batches until they are a nice golden brown and drain well on kitchen paper.

6 Serve with lemon wedges and the tartare sauce.

Tip
If your children don't like tartare sauce, try a simpler version by mixing drained sweetcorn with mayonnaise.

Baked green pesto salmon

There is nothing simpler or healthier at teatime than a lovely piece of fresh salmon. My children really enjoy salmon and it's really versatile too. Here I've topped it with a homemade pesto but it's also great in fishcakes, steamed with rice or flaked into a pasta dish.

PREP TIME 5 minutes
COOKING TIME 20 minutes
SERVES 4

For the pesto
2 large handfuls of fresh
  basil leaves
1 large garlic clove, crushed
3 tbsp pine nuts
3 tbsp extra-virgin olive oil
salt
6 tbsp freshly grated
  Parmesan

4 salmon fillets (skinless and
  boneless), approximately
  175 g (6 oz) each

1 First make the pesto. Place the basil leaves, garlic clove, pine nuts and olive oil in a food processor with a pinch of salt. Process until blended and then transfer to a mixing bowl. Mix in the grated Parmesan, adding a little more oil if the pesto is too thick. Set aside.

2 Place the salmon fillets on a baking sheet lined with aluminium foil. Spoon the pesto over the salmon, covering evenly (I like quite a thick layer).

3 Cook in a preheated oven at 220°C/425°F/gas 7 for about 12–16 minutes (the cooking time will depend on the thickness of the fillets).

4 Serve with fresh tagliatelle or new potatoes and some green vegetables.

Tip
If you prefer you can also cook the salmon under the grill – make sure the grill is not too hot or the fish will cook too quickly.

Potato wedges

I have to confess I love chips but have never managed to make a tasty healthy version at home. Wedges are a perfect alternative – by keeping the skin on you get to keep all of the goodness and vitamins. The other good thing about wedges is that you can add your own flavourings. Here I've used sweet chilli sauce but you could also try grated lemon zest, flavoured oils, finely chopped herbs (rosemary and thyme are great). If you like a bit of spice, try sprinkling them with a teaspoon of paprika before cooking.

PREP TIME 10 minutes
COOKING TIME 25 minutes
SERVES 4–6

1 kg (2 lb 2 oz) potatoes
4 tbsp sunflower oil
4 tsp sweet chilli sauce

1 Preheat the oven to 200°C/400°F/gas 6 and place a baking tray in the oven to heat up.

2 Scrub the potatoes, then cut each into half lengthways, and then each half into two or three wedges.

3 Place the potatoes in a large pan of boiling salted water and cook for about 5 minutes. Drain.

4 Tip the wedges in a large mixing bowl and drizzle over the oil and chilli sauce. Mix until all the potatoes are evenly coated.

5 Then place the potatoes on the preheated baking tray and bake on the top shelf for 15–20 minutes or until golden and crisp, turning halfway through cooking.

Perfect cheese on toast

A great teatime snack that is simple and tasty.

PREP TIME 5 minutes
COOKING TIME 5 minutes
SERVES 2

2 thick slices crusty bread
    butter, for spreading
125 g (4 oz) mature cheddar,
    sliced
4 slices honey cured ham
a few dashes Worcestershire
    sauce

1 Preheat the grill to hot and toast the bread until it is only just starting to colour on both sides.

2 Spread a little butter on each side and then lay on the slices of ham and cheese. Add a good covering of cheese – don't be shy!

3 Splash over some Worcestershire sauce and place back under the grill to cook for 2–3 minutes until golden and bubbling. Serve immediately.

Tip
For a more pepped-up version spread a thin layer of English mustard under the ham and top with freshly ground black pepper.

Hazelnut brittle

Nuts are a wonderful way for us to get quota of good fats and this recipe has become a bit of a favourite. It's a sweet and sticky treat with a little bit of goodness thrown in – perfect for an after-school nibble.

PREP TIME 5 minutes
COOKING TIME 20 minutes
MAKES about 500g (1 lb 2 oz)

300 g (10 oz) shelled
  hazelnuts
200–250 g (7–9 oz) caster
  sugar

1   Very lightly oil a baking sheet and set it on top of a chopping board.

2   Place the hazelnuts in a single layer in a baking tray and place in a cool oven (150°C/300°f/gas 2) for about 10 minutes. This is to ensure that they are fully dried out and lightly toasted. When cool, rub off any remaining skin.

3   Place the nuts and the sugar in a large heavy-based pan and heat gently over a low heat, stirring, until the sugar starts to caramelize and turn golden. Once you are happy that you have a lovely caramel colour, tip it quickly onto your baking sheet. Use a spatula to spread it out and then leave to cool.

4   When it has cooled and hardened break into pieces and store in a pretty glass jar until your next sweet craving!

Bashed into smaller fragments, this makes a great topping for ice cream.

Melt-in-the-mouth cookies

These delicious cookies are a real hit and are great to make with kids – they love rolling them in the oats. These are sold every time we have a fundraising cake stall at my children's school and they are cleared out in about 10 minutes!

PREP TIME 15 minutes
COOKING TIME 15 minutes
MAKES about 16 biscuits

150 g (5 oz) caster sugar
225 g (8 oz) butter or
   margarine
2 egg yolks
few drops vanilla essence
300 g (10 oz) self-raising flour
porridge oats
halved glacé cherries, to
   decorate (optional)

1   Preheat the oven to 180°C/350°F/gas 4. Lightly grease a couple of baking sheets (you may need to cook the cookies in batches).

2   Cream the butter and sugar together in a food processor. Add the egg yolks and vanilla extract and blend again. Add the flour, a little at a time. The mixture will start to become quite stiff, like a dough.

3   Place the oats on a large plate or shallow dish. Using clean hands, roll the mixture into small balls (about the size of a walnut). Roll each one in the oats, pressing down slightly. Flatten the balls gently and place on the baking sheets. Pop a glacé cherry half (if using) in the middle of each biscuit.

4   Bake in the oven for about 15 minutes or until golden brown. Transfer immediately to a wire cooling rack and leave to cool.

Comfort food

I'm sure you all know what I mean by comfort food – it's food that you just want to 'sink' in to. For me it's about the things I ate as a child but it has also come to mean food that I turn to again and again – when I'm feeling under the weather, when I need a bit of cheering up or even when I just want something warm and hearty on a cold winter's day. It's a very personal thing and I'm sure you have your own food memories but I hope you enjoy these recipes and that they bring comfort to you too!

Filled jackets

Jacket potatoes are the simplest of suppers and are very enjoyable for all the family. Also, if any of the children don't like your choice of filling on that particular day you can substitute something else. This tuna with a mayonnaise dressing is really tasty and light as I substitute some of the mayonnaise for crème fraîche. Ketchup gives it a lovely pinkish colour but also makes it that little bit sweeter for children.

PREP TIME 10 minutes
COOKING TIME 1 hour
SERVES 4

4 large baking potatoes, scrubbed
olive oil
400 g (14 oz) tin tuna
4 tbsp mayonnaise
4 tbsp crème fraîche,
2 tbsp tomato ketchup
1 tbsp finely chopped chives
chopped fresh parsley and paprika, to garnish

1   Preheat the oven to 220°C/475°F/gas 7.

2   Roll the potatoes lightly in some olive oil and prick them with a fork, then place them on a baking tray and cook in the oven for 50–60 minutes.

3   To prepare the filling mix the tuna in a bowl with the mayonnaise, crème fraîche, ketchup and chives. You can now cover this and leave to chill in the fridge ready for the potatoes.

4   When the potatoes are ready simply slice the open and spoon in the mixture. Sprinkle over a little parsley and some paprika.

5   Serve with a lovely fresh green salad.

The tuna also works well as a dip for crunchy vegetable sticks or you can use it to fill a crusty baguette.

Mr. Penney's potato and onion soup

I can't remember how this recipe came about – I created it one day and now it has become a regular fixture. I like the way the cardamom turns it into something special.

PREP TIME 15 minutes
COOKING TIME 45 minutes
SERVES 6

1 tbsp olive oil
2 large onions, peeled and chopped
4 cloves
6 cardamom pods, crushed and seeds removed
6 small potatoes, peeled and chopped
2 x 400 g (14 oz) tins coconut milk
400 ml (14 fl oz) water
1 vegetable stock cube
½ lime
1 tbsp chopped fresh coriander

1 Heat the oil in a large heavy-based pan and gently fry the onions until translucent (don't allow them to brown).

2 Add the cloves and cardamom seeds and cook for another 30 seconds. Add the chopped potatoes and lower the heat. Cover and cook gently for about 20 minutes, stirring to prevent from catching (remember – no liquid has been added yet).

3 Add the coconut milk, water and stock cube and bring to the boil. Simmer gently, stirring now and again to make sure the stock cube has dissolved, for about 10 minutes.

4 Squeeze the juice from lime and discard (or save for something else). Make a few cuts in the rind and then add to the pan. Cook for a further 5 minutes.

5 Remove the lime and the cloves and then transfer the soup to a blender. Blitz until almost smooth; it is better with a slightly coarse texture; a few lumps of potato don't matter.

6 Season with freshly ground pepper and reheat if necessary. To serve, sprinkle with a little chopped fresh coriander.

Dahl soup

This lentil soup is a recipe given to me by Melissa, one of the mums at our school. It's known to all as 'Melissa's gorgeous soup' and is now legendary within our community. It's shared at every school gathering and is the essence of comfort food.

PREP TIME 15 minutes
COOKING TIME 35 minutes
SERVES 6

25 g (1 oz) butter
2 garlic cloves
1 onion, peeled and chopped
½ tsp turmeric
1 tsp garam masala
¼ tsp chilli powder
1 tsp ground cumin
1 x 400 g (14 oz) tin chopped
   tomatoes
175 g (6 oz) red lentils
2 tsp lemon juice
600 ml (1 pint) vegetable
   stock
300 ml (½ pint) coconut milk
salt and freshly ground
   pepper
chopped fresh coriander
naan bread, to serve

1 Melt the butter in a large saucepan and add the garlic and onion. Cook for 2–3 minutes and then add all the spices. Cook for a further 30 seconds.

2 Stir in tomatoes, red lentils, lemon juice, vegetable stock, and coconut milk and bring to the boil.

3 Simmer for 30 minutes until lentils are tender, adding extra hot water if necessary. Season to taste and then serve sprinkled with the chopped fresh coriander. Serve with toasted naan breads for dunking in your soup.

French onion soup

This is a lovely classic soup that is great when you or your loved ones are feeling under the weather. You have to be patient and cook your onions for a long time to get that lovely dark colour.

PREP TIME 15 minutes
COOKING TIME 1 hour
SERVES 4

30 g (1 oz) butter
2 tbsp olive oil
8 large onions, peeled and
    thinly sliced
pinch dried thyme
60 ml (3 fl oz) dry white wine
    (such as Sauvignon Blanc)
1 litre (1¾ pints) vegetable or
    chicken stock
salt and freshly ground black
    pepper
100 g (3½ oz) Gruyère cheese,
    grated
8 slices French bread, toasted

1 Heat the butter and oil in a large pan over a medium heat until the butter has melted.

2 Add the onions and thyme and cook gently for about 15 minutes, taking care not to burn the onions. Reduce the heat, cover and continue cooking for 30 minutes, until the onions take on a nice rich colour. Stir occasionally.

3 Add the wine and turn up the heat to high until the wine has evaporated. Add the vegetable stock and bring to the boil. Reduce the heat and simmer for another 20 minutes. Add salt and pepper to taste.

4 Ladle the soup into four heatproof bowls, and place the toasted French bread on top and sprinkle with the cheese. (Gruyère is best but you can also use a mature cheddar.) Place the bowls under the grill until the cheese is melted and bubbling. Serve immediately.

Aunty Gwenda's minestrone

This one is a meal in itself and incredibly tasty and nourishing, particularly on a cold day after working in the garden or raking the leaves! Delicious with some warm crusty bread.

PREP TIME 20 minutes
COOKING TIME 30 minutes
SERVES 4

1 tbsp olive oil
4 rashers streaky bacon, diced
1 medium onion, peeled and chopped
1 garlic clove, peeled and crushed
1 carrot, diced
1 small turnip, peeled and diced
2 sticks celery, chopped
1 leek, sliced
2 tsp chopped fresh parsley
2 tbsp tomato purée
2 large tomatoes, skinned and chopped
900 ml (1½ pints) chicken stock
salt and freshly ground black pepper
30 g (1 oz) spaghetti, broken into short lengths
¼ green cabbage, finely shredded
1 tbsp grated Parmesan

1 Heat the oil in a large heavy-based pan and fry the bacon until the fat runs out. Add the onions and garlic and cook until golden brown. Then stir in the carrot, turnip, celery, leek and parsley and cook for 5 minutes.

2 Add the tomato purée, tomatoes, stock and salt and pepper. Bring to the boil and then cover and simmer for 10–15 minutes.

3 Add the spaghetti and check the seasoning. Stir well and cook for a further 8 minutes. Add the shredded cabbage 5 minutes before the end of the cooking time.

4 To serve pour into bowls and sprinkle with Parmesan.

My Mum's sausage and bean casserole

Mum had a particular talent for rustling up something tasty and reasonably healthy on a very tight budget – in fact it often felt like no budget at all. I think this recipe is a great example of making the most of the few things that were often left in a fridge or a half empty cupboard.

PREP TIME 10 minutes
COOKING TIME 40 minutes
SERVES 4–5

1 tbsp olive oil
2 onions, peeled and chopped
3 rashers smoked bacon, diced
8–10 good-quality sausages
2 x 400 g (14 oz) tins baked beans
2 tbsp tomato purée
1 tbsp brown sugar
½ tsp dry mustard
2–3 tsp Worcestershire sauce
¼ tsp mixed herbs
150 ml (5 fl oz) water
salt and freshly ground black pepper

To serve
chopped fresh parsley
warm bread

1   Preheat the oven to 180°C/350°F/gas 4.

2   Heat the oil in a large casserole dish and add the chopped onion. Fry gently for about 5 minutes and then add the bacon and sausages and brown all over.

3   Add the rest of the ingredients and bring to the boil. Cover and cook in the oven for about 30 minutes.

4   Sprinkle with some chopped fresh parsley and serve with warm bread.

Sweet carrots

This is a great side dish and one that we eat a lot as my children love carrots, plus it works with so many different dishes. If you're feeling more adventurous try adding a pinch or two of ground coriander or cumin to add a little spice.

PREP TIME 10 minutes
COOKING TIME 20 minutes
SERVES 4

700 g (1 1/2 lb) carrots, peeled
    and cut into sticks
2 tbsp olive oil
salt and freshly ground black
    pepper
1 tbsp runny honey

1   Preheat oven to 180°C/350°F/gas 4 and place a sheet of aluminium foil in a large baking tray.

2   Place the prepared carrots in a large mixing bowl and add the oil and salt and pepper. Drizzle over the honey and toss or stir the carrots until they are all coated in the oil and honey.

3   Tip the carrots on to the foil-lined baking tray and spread out in a single layer. Bake in the oven for 20 minutes or until the carrots are tender.

Butternut and red onion tart

This is a 'tarte tatin' style dish, showing that the method works just as well for savoury dishes. A lovely winter warmer.

PREP TIME 20 minutes
COOKING TIME 40 minutes
SERVES 6

2 tbsp olive oil
1.5 kg (3 lb 5 oz) butternut
   squash, peeled, deseeded
   and cut into chunks
6 tomatoes, halved
120 g (4 oz) butter
4 red onions, peeled and
   cut into wedges
5 garlic cloves, peeled and
   finely chopped
1 red chilli, deseeded and
   chopped
1 tsp ground coriander
1 tsp ground cumin
1 packet ready-rolled
   puff pastry
1 egg whisked with 1 tbsp
   cold water

1 Preheat the oven to 220°C/425°F/gas 7. Place 1 tbsp olive oil in a large baking tray and add the butternut squash. Toss to coat in the oil and then make sure the squash is in a single layer so that it cooks evenly. Cook in the oven for about 10–15 minutes – you're just looking for them to soften a little.

2 Two minutes before the squash is ready add the tomatoes, cut side down.

3 Meanwhile melt the butter and the remaining oil in a pan. Add the onion, garlic and chilli. Cook for about 4–5 minutes. Stir in the coriander and cumin and fry for a minute longer.

4 Tip the onion, garlic and chilli into the baking tray with the squash, making sure it is evenly distributed. Leave to cool.

5 Roll out the pastry making one sheet large enough to cover the whole tray. Lay the sheet over your vegetables and trim off the excess. Place in the fridge to chill for about 30 minutes.

6 Brush the pastry with the egg and bake in the oven for about 20 minutes. Ovens may vary so keep an eye on the pastry throughout; you are looking for a golden brown pastry and the juices bubbling around the edges. Remove from the oven and place a tray or board over the baking tray. Carefully flip the baking tray over and serve immediately.

Baked macaroni cheese

Here is a recipe for a delicious pasta bake. It's really simple to make and I usually do it late afternoon before collecting the children from school then move it into a cool oven until the kids arrive. Our macaroni is a guaranteed hit – not because of the rave reviews from the kids but more because without fail their plates are also emptied!

PREP TIME 10 minutes
COOKING TIME 35 minutes
SERVES 4

200 g (7 oz) dried macaroni
50 g (2 oz) butter
50 g (2 oz) plain flour
600 ml (1 pint) milk
225 g (8 oz) cheddar
salt and freshly ground
  black pepper
2 tbsp fresh breadcrumbs

1 Preheat the oven to 180°C/350°F/gas 4. Cook the macaroni as per your packets instructions. Drain, rinse in cold water (to stop it sticking together) and return to the pan.

2 Melt the butter in a pan over a low heat. Add the flour and cook, stirring, for about 1 minute.

3 Remove the pan from the heat and stir in your milk slowly, a little at a time. Then place it back on the heat and slowly bring to the boil, it must be stirred almost continuously to stop it sticking.

4 Once the sauce thickens and starts to bubble you can take it off the heat and stir in your cheese (keep some back to sprinkle on top). Season to taste. Pour the sauce over your macaroni and mix it in really well. Evie is very quick to point out when her 'pasta isn't very creamy today'.

5 Tip the macaroni into a large ovenproof dish. Mix the rest of the grated cheddar with the breadcrumbs and scatter over the top of the macaroni. Bake it in the oven for about 25 minutes or until it is a lovely golden brown.

Mixing grated cheese with breadcrumbs gives a lovely crunchy topping to this simple but delicious dish.

Salmon and leek bake

This lovely dish is perfect on a cold day.

PREP TIME 20 minutes
COOKING TIME 30 minutes
SERVES 4

1 tbsp of olive oil
450 g (1 lb) skinless and
    boneless salmon fillet
4 medium leeks, sliced
600 g (1 lb 5 oz) potatoes,
    peeled and halved

For the sauce
40 g (1½ oz) butter
40 g (1½ oz) plain flour
400 ml (14 fl oz) milk
110 g (4 oz) cheddar, grated
salt and freshly ground
    black pepper
1 tbsp chopped fresh parsley

1   First cook the salmon. Preheat the oven to
    180°C/350°F/gas 4. Place a large piece of foil on a
    baking tray and place the salmon fillet on top. Season
    with pepper and fold the foil over to make a loose
    parcel. Cook in the oven for about 15 minutes,
    depending on the thickness of the fillet.

2   Heat the oil in a pan and add the leeks. Fry gently for a
    couple of minutes and then tip them into an ovenproof
    dish. Flake the cooked salmon and add to the leeks.

3   Meanwhile cook the potatoes until just tender, about
    10 minutes. Slice thickly and arrange the potato slices
    on top of the salmon and leeks.

4   To make the sauce melt the butter in a pan, add the
    plain flour and cook for a couple of minutes. Gradually
    stir in the milk and bring to the boil, stirring all the time.
    Remove from the heat and stir in the cheese, keeping a
    little back for the topping. Season to taste.

5   Pour the sauce over the potatoes and sprinkle over the
    remaining cheese. Return to the oven and cook for a
    further 10–15 minutes until the top turns a nice golden
    colour. Serve scattered with the chopped fresh parsley.

Creamy mashed potato

Mashed potato has to be the ultimate comfort food and certainly seems to warm the coldest cockles on a wintry Sunday afternoon – or any afternoon for that matter. I use white pepper for a really smooth perfect mash – without any 'bits'.

PREP TIME 15 minutes
COOKING TIME 25 minutes
SERVES 4

1 kg (2 lb 3 oz) floury potatoes,
   such as maris piper
100 ml (3½ fl oz) single cream
75 g (2½ oz) butter (at room
   temperature)
freshly grated nutmeg
salt and ground white
   pepper

1   First, peel the potatoes and cut into equal-sized chunks. Place in a large pan of water and add a good pinch of salt, cover and bring to the boil.

2   When it has reached boiling point, remove the lid and cook the potatoes for a further 20 minutes until they are soft and tender. Try not to over boil the potatoes or will you will have soggy wet mash!

3   While the potatoes are cooking, put the cream, butter and a pinch of grated nutmeg into a small pan and heat gently until the butter has melted. You will have a much creamier mash if you do this.

4   Drain the potatoes thoroughly, leaving them in the colander for a few minutes so the steam evaporates. Tip back into the pan and mash, adding the warm buttery cream as you go. Season with salt and a little pepper to taste.

Tip
Mash is so versatile and you can add different flavourings too. Try crushed garlic, finely chopped herbs, grated cheese or a dollop of pesto.

Toad in the hole

Sausages and crispy batter – what a perfect combination. I like to use smaller chipolatas.

PREP TIME 10 minutes
COOKING TIME 40 minutes
SERVES 4

1 tbsp vegetable oil
450 g (1 lb) good-quality
    pork sausages

For the batter
125 g (4 oz) plain flour
pinch of salt
1 egg
300 ml (½ pint) milk
1 tbsp chopped fresh parsley
1 tbsp chopped fresh
    rosemary or thyme

1 Preheat the oven to 220°C/425°F/gas 7. Heat the oil in a medium roasting tray on the hob, tilting the tin to oil the sides. Add the sausages and place in the oven for 10 minutes, or until the sausages are just browned and the fat is very hot.

2 Meanwhile, make the batter. Sift the flour and salt in a bowl. Make a well in the centre and add the egg with a little of the milk. Whisk the eggs and milk together, gradually drawing in the flour from around the sides. Add the remaining milk and chopped herbs, stirring all the time. Beat for a couple of minutes to make a smooth batter.

3 Reduce the oven temperature to 200°C/400°F/gas 6. Pour the batter into the roasting tin around the sausages and cook for a further 30 minutes, or until the batter is well risen, golden and crisp.

Melinda's yummy lamb hot pot

A simple hot pot that is so tasty due to the lamb being allowed to cook for a long period. Try and prepare it around midday and leave to cook until tea time. This dish is lovely on a cold winter's day and it can be popped into the oven and be ready for you when you return home from a wintry walk.

PREP TIME 10 minutes
COOKING TIME 2½–3 hours
SERVES 4

2 tbsp olive oil
900 g (2 lb) middle neck of
   lamb, cut into large chunks
2 onions, peeled and finely
   chopped
3 large carrots, peeled and
   sliced
4 large potatoes, peeled and
   thinly sliced
salt and freshly ground
   black pepper
400 ml (14 fl oz) hot chicken
   or lamb stock

1 Preheat the oven to 180°C/350°F/gas 4. Heat the oil in a large heavy-based casserole dish and brown the lamb in batches. Remove from the pan and set aside.

2 Add the onions and carrots to the pan and fry gently until soft and golden, about 5 minutes. Return the browned lamb and turn off the heat.

3 Arrange the potatoes in neat layer on top of the meat and carrots, overlapping the potato slices as you go and adding plenty of salt and pepper. Pour the hot stock over the potatoes until the potatoes are just covered. Cover with a tight-fitting lid or with foil and cook in the oven for about 2–2½ hours.

Desserts

I'd be lying if I said that I make homemade desserts like the ones in this chapter every day – a lot of the time it's fruit and yogurt for 'afters'. But I do love a good pudding and it's great to be able to turn to a few failsafe recipes for weekends, special occasions and those days when you just crave something sweet. Some parents I know are quite strict about treats but I'm a firm believer in 'a little bit of what you like does you good'. As long as my children are eating plenty of other healthy foods, I'm happy. So tuck in!

Mini strawberry pavlovas

This is a great one for kids and they can put this together easily themselves. If you want to make your own meringue see page 134 but if you're pressed for time just buy good-quality meringue nests from the supermarket. And of course, you can vary the fruit, depending on what's in season – sliced nectarines, kiwi fruit, raspberries and blueberries are all delicious.

PREP TIME 5 minutes
SERVES 4

4 meringue nests
400 ml (14 fl oz) double cream
400 g (14 oz) strawberries
1 tbsp caster sugar

1 First wash and hull the strawberries and then halve or slice (depending on the size).

2 Whip the cream until stiff and then pile into the meringue nests. Top with the sliced strawberries and then sprinkle each with a little caster sugar.

3 Alternatively you can serve this as the traditional pudding 'Eton Mess'. Simply crush the meringues roughly and pile into a bowl with the sliced strawberries and whipped cream. Stir through and serve immediately.

Granny's baked Alaska

I'm using many recipes passed down from my Granny in this book and this is without doubt our family's favourite pudding. However, as expected no-one seems to cook it like Granny used to!

PREP TIME 15 minutes
COOKING TIME 4 minutes
SERVES 4–6

1 x ready-made sponge
   flan case
600 ml (1 pint) vanilla
   ice cream (in a block)
5 egg whites
8 oz caster sugar
100 g (3½ oz) blueberries
100 g (3½ oz) raspberries

1   Preheat the oven to 230°C/450°F/gas 8 and line a baking tray with greaseproof paper.

2   Put the sponge on the baking tray and place the ice cream block onto the sponge case. Trim the sponge around the ice cream, leaving a 2 cm (¾ in) border all round. Return the ice cream to the freezer. Pile the fruit on top of the ice cream and return the

3   Whisk the egg whites until 'pearly' and then add half the sugar and whisk again. Fold in the remaining sugar.

4   Working quickly, assemble the baked Alaska. Put the ice cream on top of the sponge and then cover with the fruit. Pile the meringue over the top and sides, making sure there are no gaps. Bake in the oven for 3–4 minutes until just golden brown. Serve immediately.

Mixed berry and lemon pavlova

When I first made this recipe it went straight to the top of the charts. Pavlova is a really good dessert to serve when you have friends over – most people love meringue, especially one topped with fresh fruit. It's also great because you can make the meringue in advance – just store in an airtight container.

PREP TIME 20 minutes, plus cooling
COOKING TIME 1½ hours
SERVES 6

4 egg whites
225 g (8 oz) caster sugar
1 tsp cornflour
splash of lemon juice
grated zest of 1 lemon

For the topping
150 ml (5 fl oz) double cream, whipped
1 tbsp of icing sugar
250 ml (9 fl oz) mixed berry yogurt
splash of lemon juice
200 g (7 oz) strawberries (sliced or whole)
200 g (7 oz) blueberries
200 g (7 oz) raspberries

1 Preheat the oven to 110°C/225°F/gas ¼. Line a baking sheet with baking parchment and mark out a circle, approximately 25 cm (10 in) in diameter on the paper.

2 Whisk the egg whites until 'pearly' and then add half the sugar. Whisk again and then fold in the remaining sugar. Then add the cornflour, lemon juice and finally the zest.

3 Pile the meringue onto the circle and spread into a round shape. Hollow out the centre so that the sides are higher. Bake in the oven for 1½–2 hours. For best results turn off the oven and leave the pavlova in the oven to cool. Pavlova should be crisp on the outside and still slightly gooey in the middle. When it's ready you can peel off the parchment and get it on your serving plate – don't worry too much if the meringue cracks a little.

4 Mix the cream, icing sugar, yogurt and lemon juice together and then place this onto your meringue. Top with the fruit, halving the strawberries if necessary. Serve immediately, with some extra cream on the side for those who want it.

Clementine and apricot pudding

I like to use Manuka honey in this recipe – it is expensive but has wonderful health-giving properties. But any good runny honey would do.

PREP TIME 5 minutes
COOKING TIME 10 minutes
SERVES 4

10 ripe apricots, washed
   and halved
250 ml (9 fl oz) fresh orange
   juice
2 tsp honey
few drops vanilla essence
6–8 clementines, peeled,
   pith removed
200 g (7 oz) white grapes
Greek yogurt or vanilla ice
   cream, to serve

1 Place the apricots in a pan and add the orange juice, honey and vanilla essence. Simmer gently for about 10 minutes. The fruit needs to be soft but still keep its shape.

2 Remove from the heat and transfer to a serving dish. Divide the clementines into segments and add to the apricots along with the grapes. Chill in the refrigerator.

3 Serve with Greek yogurt if you're being good, vanilla ice cream if you're feeling naughty!

Creamy rice pudding

Most children love a creamy rice pudding. and you can serve it with jam, honey or fruit to give it that little something extra.

PREP TIME 10 minutes
COOKING TIME 1½ hours
SERVES 4

1 litre (1¾ pints) semi-
    skimmed milk
4 tbsp sugar
140 g (5 oz) pudding rice
600 ml fresh cream
1 tsp vanilla essence
2 tbsp caster sugar
1 tsp ground cinnamon

1   Bring the milk and sugar to the boil in a large pan. Add the rice, cover, reduce the heat and simmer until the rice absorbs all the milk. This may take anything up to 1½ hours so cook very gently and stir occasionally to make sure the rice isn't sticking to the pan. Set aside to cool slightly.

2   Meanwhile whip the cream gently until thick. Add to the rice mixture along with the vanilla essence.

3   Pour the rice pudding into heatproof serving bowls and sprinkle with the caster sugar and a little cinnamon. Place under a preheated grill for a few moments until the topping is golden.

4   Leave to cool slightly before serving – alternatively you can let it go cold and refrigerate before serving.

Baked apples

Bramley apples work best for this great autumn dessert. Pick nice round ones that are evenly sized.

PREP TIME 10 minutes
COOKING TIME 40 minutes
SERVES 4

1 tbsp raisins
4 tbsp orange juice
4 large cooking apples,
    washed and cored
8 cloves
50 g (2 oz) butter
2 tbsp brown sugar
1 tsp ground cinnamon
cream, custard or ice cream,
    to serve

1   In a bowl mix the raisins and orange juice. Use a sharp knife to cut through the skin of each apple, around its middle. Place the apples in an ovenproof dish and stuff the core of each one with the raisin and juice mix.

2   Stick a couple of cloves into each apple and place a quarter of the butter on the top of each apple. Sprinkle with the brown sugar and cinnamon.

3   Bake in the oven for 30–40 minutes, adding a little water to the dish if it looks like the apples are drying out.

4   Serve with thick cream, custard or a dollop of ice cream.

Gorgeous caramel apple crumble

A little twist on a traditional pudding. You can find caramel sauce in most good supermarkets – often near the ice cream section.

PREP TIME 10 minutes
COOKING TIME 40 minutes
SERVES 4

4 large eating apples,
   peeled and sliced
100 g (3½ oz) dark brown
   sugar
2 tbsp caramel sauce
175 g (6 oz) plain flour
125 g (4 oz) caster sugar
1 tsp ground cinnamon
1 egg, beaten
50 g (2 oz) butter, melted
2 tbsp granulated sugar

1 Preheat the oven to 190°C/375°F/gas 5.

2 Mix the sliced apples with the caramel sauce and the brown sugar and layer in an ovenproof dish, approximately 23 cm (9 in) square.

3 Place the flour, caster sugar and ground cinnamon together in a large bowl and mix together. In a separate bowl beat together the egg and melted butter. Then stir in the flour mixture.

4 Spoon the crumble mixture evenly over the apples and sprinkle with the granulated sugar.

5 Bake in the oven for 30–40 minutes, or until the topping is golden and crisp.

Almond and pear tart

This is an absolutely delicious tart. You can use fresh pears but they can be too hard so I've suggested a quick option using tinned pears. Pastry dough freezes really well so double up on the ingredients if you want and freeze half for another time.

PREP TIME 25 minutes, plus chilling
COOKING TIME 45–50 minutes
SERVES 6

For the pastry
175 g (6 oz) plain flour
pinch of salt
100 g (3½ oz) unsalted butter, diced
50 g (2 oz) caster sugar
1 egg yolk
1 tbsp cold water

For the filling
120 g (4 oz) unsalted butter
100 g (3½ oz) caster sugar
2 eggs, beaten
25 g (1 oz) plain flour
125 g (4½ oz) ground almonds
1 x 400 g (4 oz) tin pear halves
2 tbsp sliced almonds

1 First make the pastry. Sift the flour and salt into a bowl and rub in the butter until you have something that looks like fine breadcrumbs. Add the sugar and mix through, then add the egg yolk and a little water. Mix to form a soft dough. Knead lightly, wrap in cling film and refrigerate for about 30 minutes.

2 Preheat the oven to 180°C/350°F/gas 4. Lightly grease a 23 cm (9 in) loose-bottomed flan tin. Roll out the pastry on a lightly floured surface until you have a circle large enough to cover the tin. Press gently into the tin, prick the base with a fork and trim away the excess.

3 Line the pastry with non-stick baking paper and baking beans and bake 'blind' for about 10 minutes. Remove the beans and paper and return to the oven for a further 5–10 minutes.

4 Cream the butter and sugar until light and fluffy and then gradually beat in the eggs. Add the flour and almonds and beat gently. Spoon the almond mixture into the prepared pastry case.

5 Drain the pears and arrange them on top of the filling, pointed ends towards the centre. Scatter with sliced almonds and return to the oven for about 25–30 minutes, until it is nice and golden.

6 Serve warm. This is delicious with simple chocolate sauce – just melt about 150 g (5 oz) good-quality chocolate and add about 110 ml (3 fl oz) double cream.

White chocolate parfait with a fresh fruit sauce

This is really simple to create and if you use ready-made meringue nests involves no cooking (just a bit of melting). A great one to prepare in advance.

PREP TIME 20 minutes, plus chilling
SERVES 6

280 ml (10 fl oz) double cream
200 ml (7 fl oz) Greek yogurt
4 meringue nests
200 g (7 oz) white chocolate, melted

For the sauce
150 g (5 oz) raspberries (reserve a few to decorate)
150 g (5 oz) strawberries
2 tbsp icing sugar
1 tbsp lemon juice

1 Pour the cream into a large bowl and whisk until you form soft peaks. Melt the white chocolate in a bowl over a pan of simmering water.

2 Break the meringue nests into small pieces and then fold into the cream along with the white chocolate and the yogurt.

3 Take 6 ramekins or small dessert glasses and line each one with cling film. Spoon the mixture into each ramekin, pushing down firmly. Fold the cling film over and then place them in the freezer for approximately 2 hours.

4 To make the sauce put the raspberries, strawberries, lemon juice and icing sugar into a blender and blend into a purée. Pass the sauce through a sieve to remove the seeds.

5 When you are ready to serve remove the ramekins from the freezer and turn out onto plates. Garnish with a few raspberries and serve with the sauce.

If you want a pretty marbled effect, swirl some of the sauce through the parfait mixture before placing in the ramekins.

Crunchy chocolate delight

This dessert may not be quite so easy on the waistline but it is certainly worth the guilt trip. However, I would suggest that you serve in small portions – little glasses or ramekins work well. An indulgent treat! It's inspired by a dessert my stepmother Teresa makes for us and has become a family favourite.

PREP TIME 15 minutes,
 plus chilling
SERVES 6

225 g (8 oz) milk chocolate
2 Crunchie bars
300 ml (10 fl oz) double cream
250 g (9 oz) mascarpone

1 Grate or shave a little of your chocolate to keep back for decoration. Put the remainder in a heatproof bowl and place over a pan of gently simmering water until melted.

2 Place the Crunchie bars in plastic bag and use a rolling pin to smash them up – the kids usually like helping with this bit! Tip the Crunchie pieces into the melted chocolate and stir through.

3 In a separate bowl mix together the cream and mascarpone. Beat until smooth. Add the chocolate mixture and stir through – I like a nice swirly effect so I don't mix it too thoroughly. Spoon into your serving dishes, decorate with the chocolate shavings and chill for about 20 minutes before serving.

Chocolate mousse

Chocolate mousse is a classic dessert – definitely one for the chocolate lovers.
I use a good-quality dark chocolate but you can also experiment with flavoured
chocolate, such as mint or orange. These look great served in little espresso
cups, perhaps dusted with icing sugar or cocoa powder or topped with a fresh
raspberry or two.

PREP TIME 15 minutes,
plus chilling
SERVES 6–8

175 g (6 oz) good-quality
plain chocolate
115 g (4 oz) caster sugar
5 eggs, separated
2 tbsp double cream
cocoa powder, for dusting

1   Break up the chocolate, place in a pan and heat gently
until the chocolate has melted. Add the sugar and stir
until dissolved.

2   Remove from the heat and beat in the egg yolks. Mix
until light and fluffy.

3   In a separate bowl whisk the egg whites and then gently
fold into the chocolate mixture. Pour into small pots or
espresso cups, cool and then chill in the refrigerator for
at least for hours or overnight.

4   To serve, swirl with a little double cream and dust with
cocoa powder.

Banoffee toffee pots

This dessert is so tasty and easy – it's a bit of a cheat's recipe. I like to serve in small sundae glasses so you can make each portion as small or big as you like.

PREP TIME 10 minutes
SERVES 4

about 6 digestive biscuits
ready-made toffee sauce
2 bananas, sliced
300 ml (10 fl oz) whipping
   cream
50 g (2 oz) milk chocolate

1   Place the biscuits in a food bag and use a rolling pin to smash into crumbs.

2   Divide the biscuit crumbs between the serving glasses (you should have about 2 cm / 1 in in each glass).

3   Squeeze a layer of toffee sauce on each biscuit layer – don't worry about making it too neat.

4   Now top with the sliced banana slices. Softly whip the cream and spread over the bananas. Finish by sprinkling with chocolate shavings. You can use a vegetable peeler or cheese grate for this (kids love doing this, but make sure you don't lose too much chocolate in the process!)

Baking

Most children love baking – there is something quite magical about turning simple ingredients such as flour, eggs and yeast into delicious breads and cakes. I love it when the kitchen is filled with the smell of freshly baked bread and when we make fairy cakes there is no stopping my kids when it comes to the decorating. They're pretty good at eating them too!

Mum's lemon drizzle

Possibly the easiest cake in the world to make! And a very good one to get the kids involved with. If your children don't want it quite this traditional and basic try mixing up an icing also and maybe have some sweets or jellies to decorate it.

PREP TIME 15 minutes
COOKING TIME 25–30 minutes
SERVES 8

160 g (5½ oz) self-raising flour
1 tsp baking powder
160 g (5½ oz) caster sugar
120 g (4 oz) butter
2 eggs
4 tbsp milk
1 tbsp grated lemon rind (unwaxed lemons are best for this)

For the drizzle
130 g (4½ oz) caster sugar
juice of 1 lemon

1 Preheat the oven to 180°C/350°F/gas 4. Lightly grease a 20 cm (8 in) square tin and line with greaseproof paper.

2 Beat the butter and sugar together, either in a large bowl or food processor. Add the eggs and half the flour and mix. Add the remaining flour and the rest of the ingredients and beat until smooth.

3 Tip the mixture into your prepared tin and bake in the oven for about 25–30 minutes. Meanwhile whisk together the lemon juice and caster sugar.

4 Remove the cake from the oven and leave to cool in the tin for 5 minutes. Turn out onto a wire cooling tray and turn the right way up. Pour the lemon drizzle over while the cake is still warm so it soaks into the cake. Leave to cool before serving – the drizzle should have cooled into a delicious sugary 'crust'.

Gingerbread

This delicious recipe came from the mother of a very good friend of ours, Christian. It's delicious spread with a little butter.

PREP TIME 15 minutes
COOKING TIME 1½ hours
SERVES 8–10

3 tbsp black treacle
3 tbsp golden syrup
75 g (3 oz) sugar
1 tbsp chunky marmalade
175 g (6 oz) butter
340 g (12 oz) plain flour
2 tsp ground ginger
1 tsp mixed spice
1 tsp bicarbonate of soda
pinch of salt
2 eggs, beaten
150 ml (5 fl oz), plus 4 tbsp
   milk

1 Preheat the oven to 180°C/350°F/gas 4. Lightly grease a 20 cm (8 in) square tin and line with greaseproof paper.

2 Put the treacle, syrup, sugar, marmalade and butter in a pan. Heat gently until all the ingredients are melted.

3 Sift the flour, ginger, mixed spice, bicarbonate of soda and salt into a large mixing bowl and make a well in the centre. Pour the melted butter mixture into the middle and add the beaten eggs and milk. Stir gently, starting in the middle and drawing the flour in from the sides. Beat for a few minutes until all the ingredients are well combined and then pour into your prepared tin.

4 Bake in the centre of the oven for about 1½ hours until cooked. Allow to cool in the tin for 5 minutes before turning out onto a cooling rack.

Melinda's fabulous fairy cakes

These cakes disappear as quickly as they are put out – everyone loves them and they always look fabulous. The magic of fairy cakes is that they are so simple and quick to make, and there are so many different ways to make them taste and look great. This is a simple recipe, but the effort is in the decoration. I use wholemeal flour but you can easily substitute plain white flour. The method may seem too straightforward – at school I was taught to painstakingly cream the butter, sugar and eggs and then slowly fold in the flour to 'trap the air'. But I promise you this way works – perhaps it's the magic ingredient, baking powder.

PREP TIME 20 minutes
COOKING TIME 15 minutes
MAKES about 20

4 eggs
225 g (8 oz) wholemeal
   self-raising flour
225 g (8 oz) golden caster
   sugar
225 g (8 oz) butter
pinch of salt
1 drop of vanilla essence
1 tbsp baking powder

For the topping
175 g (6 oz) icing sugar
110 g (4 oz) butter
few drops of flavouring
   (optional)
food colouring
1–2 tbsp milk
decorations (see right)

1 Preheat the oven to 180°C/350°F/gas 4.

2 Place all the ingredients together in a food processor and mix together until light and fluffy.

3 Spoon the mixture into cake cases – you want them to be about one third full. Place them in the oven for about 15 minutes until the tops are golden. To test if they are done insert a skewer into the cakes, if it comes out clean then they are ready.

4 While the cakes are cooling, prepare your butter icing. Beat the butter in a large bowl until soft. Add half the icing sugar and beat until smooth. Then add the remaining icing sugar with one tablespoon of the milk. Beat until creamy then add a few drops of food colouring and any flavouring if using. I like unusual flavours like lilac and rose but orange, vanilla, strawberry and lemon are more popular with children. Add extra icing sugar to thicken or a little extra milk to make more runny if necessary.

5 Some of the cakes may rise more in the middle; cut the bumps off with a sharp knife before decorating them. Either use a knife to spread the icing onto the cakes, or pipe it on. Be as generous as you want.

6 Now to make your cakes look fabulous! Choose from fresh halved strawberries, sweeties, crystallized flower petals – even edible glitter.

Welsh cakes

As Wayne is Welsh I could not resist including some of his family's finest offerings! This recipe is from Wayne's mum and it is absolutely delicious. Welsh cakes would traditionally be cooked on a large cast-iron griddle but a large frying pan works just as well. They are a more than equal alternative to scones and can be served in the same way – hot, cold, with jam, with butter, with both! I love them hot...

PREP TIME 15 minutes
COOKING TIME 5 minutes
MAKES about 20

450 g (1 lb) plain flour
1 tsp baking powder
pinch of salt
170 g (6 oz) butter, diced
170 g (6 oz) caster sugar
170 g (6 oz) mixed currants
   and sultanas
1 egg, beaten
about 3–4 tbsp milk
extra caster sugar, for serving

1 Sift together the flour, baking powder and salt. Add in the butter and rub in with your fingers until the mixture resembles fine breadcrumbs.

2 Add the sugar and fruit. Mix in the egg and just enough milk to make it the same consistency as short-crust pastry.

3 Now place onto a floured board and roll out to a thickness of about 1 cm ($\frac{1}{2}$ in). Using an 8 cm (3 in) pastry cutter, cut into round shapes.

4 Lightly grease and warm a heavy-based pan over a medium heat. When the pan is hot, cook the cakes for about 3–4 minutes on each side. If they brown too quickly you need to lower the heat. When cooked, they will have a crumbly, scone like texture inside. Sprinkle a little sugar on to taste.

Serve either hot or cold with butter and jam.

Chocolate orange buns

These cute little cupcakes are great for a quick chocolate hit.

PREP TIME 15 minutes
COOKING TIME 20 minutes
MAKES about 16

200 g (7 oz) self-raising flour
225 g (8 oz) caster sugar
2 tbsp cocoa powder
pinch of salt
115 g (4 oz) butter
2 eggs
finely grated rind of 1 orange
5 tbsp condensed milk
5 tbsp orange juice

For the buttercream
50 g (2 oz) butter
115 g (4 oz) icing sugar
1 tbsp cocoa powder
finely grated rind of 1 orange

1 Preheat the oven to 180°C/350°F/gas 4.

2 Sieve all the dry ingredients into a bowl. Rub in the butter until it resembles fine breadcrumbs.

3 Beat together the eggs, orange rind, condensed milk and orange juice. Add to the dry ingredients and beat well.

4 Spoon the mixture into cake cases and cook in the oven for 15–20 minutes. Meanwhile make the chocolate buttercream by beating together the butter, sugar, cocoa and orange rind. When the cakes are cool, top with the buttercream.

Chocolate brownies

These delicious brownies are really easy to make. I always look for good-quality organic cocoa powder. We like these just as they are but you can try adding chopped walnuts, pecans or chocolate chunks to the mixture before baking.

PREP TIME 10 minutes
COOKING TIME 20–30 minutes
MAKES about 12

125 g (4 oz) butter or margarine, softened
225 g (8 oz) granulated sugar
50 g (2 oz) self-raising flour
50 g (2 oz) cocoa powder
2 eggs, beaten

1 Preheat the oven to 180°C/350°F/gas 4. Lightly grease a 25 x 17 cm (10 x 7 in) baking tin and line the bottom with greaseproof paper.

2 Cream the butter or margarine by hand or in a food processor (having the butter at room temperature will make this easier).

3 Add the flour, cocoa and beaten eggs and blend again. Take care not to overmix.

4 Pour the mixture into the prepared tin and bake in the oven for 20–30 minutes. Remove from the oven and leave to cool in the tin for 5 minutes. Turn on to a wire cooling tray and remove the paper. Allow to cool completely before cutting into squares.

Beetroot and chocolate cake

This is another wonderful recipe given to me by one of the mums at our school. Jo is a very good friend of mine but before she came to our school she lived in New Zealand and this recipe was given to her by the mothers of the Takapuna Playcentre in Auckland shortly after the birth of her second child – the beetroot means that it is an excellent pick-me-up after childbirth. It's absolutely delicious – chocolatey, rich and a gorgeous colour but nutritious as well. I have yet to find anyone who doesn't like it.

PREP TIME 20 minutes
COOKING TIME 55 minutes
SERVES 6–8

225 g (8 oz) plain flour
2 tsp baking powder
pinch salt
25 g (1 oz) cocoa powder
2 eggs
150 g (5 oz) caster sugar
125 ml (4½ fl oz) vegetable oil
grated rind of 1 orange
juice of ½ orange
150 g (5 oz) cooked beetroot,
    grated
200 g (7 oz) chocolate chips
icing sugar, for dusting

1 Preheat the oven to 180°C/350°F/gas 4. Lightly grease and line a 20 cm (8 in) round cake tin.

2 Sieve the flour, baking powder, salt and cocoa into a large mixing bowl.

3 In a separate bowl beat the eggs and sugar together until light and fluffy. Add the oil, orange rind, juice and grated beetroot and beat well. Take a moment to admire the colour!

4 Gently fold in the dry ingredients until well combined. Then stir in the chocolate chips.

5 Turn into your prepared tin and bake in the oven for 50–55 minutes. Leave to cool in the tin for about 10 minutes before turning out onto a cooling rack.

6 To serve, dust with a little icing sugar.

Pineapple fruit loaf

Pineapple is a great addition to a fruit cake as it gives a lovely sweetness and texture. This is a lovely afternoon tea treat and if you're feeling particularly indulgent you can spread a little butter on each slice.

PREP TIME 15 minutes
COOKING TIME 1 hour
SERVES 6–8

175 g (6 oz) butter
175 g (6 oz) brown sugar
450 g (1 lb) mixed dried fruit
200 g (7 oz) glacé cherries
175 g (6 oz) tinned crushed
    pineapple, drained
340 g (12 oz) self-raising flour
2 eggs, beaten

1   Preheat the oven to 160°C/320°F/gas 3. Grease and line a 20 x 10 cm (8 x 4 in) loaf tin.

2   Put the butter and sugar in a large pan over a medium heat and stir slowly. When the butter has melted and the sugar has dissolved, add the dried fruit, cherries and drained pineapple and stir through. Heat gently for a couple of minutes.

3   Sieve the flour into a large mixing bowl and make a well in the centre. Add the buttery fruit mixture and beaten eggs and stir well to combine all the ingredients.

4   Pour the mixture into your prepared tin and bake in the oven for 1 hour, or until a skewer inserted into the cake comes out clean. Leave to cool in the tin for 5 minutes before turning out onto a wire rack. Leave to cool completely before removing the lining paper.

Christmas cake

This is another favourite recipe handed down from the mother of a friend. Apparently in Yorkshire, they eat this Christmas cake with a large slice of crumbly cheese!

PREP TIME 20 minutes
COOKING TIME 3–4 hours
SERVES 10–12

500 g (1 lb 2 oz) mixed
    dried fruit
500 g (1 lb 2 oz) raisins
1 × 227 g (8 oz) tin crushed
    pineapple, drained
200 g (7 oz) glacé cherries
285 g (10 oz) self-raising flour
½ tsp mixed spice
½ tsp ground cinnamon
55 g (2 oz) ground almonds
55 g (2 oz) chopped brazil nuts
175 g (6 oz) butter, melted
175 g (6 oz) soft brown sugar
1 tbsp treacle
1 tbsp golden syrup
5 eggs, beaten
3 tbsp brandy (optional)

1   Preheat the oven to 165°C/325°F/gas 3. Grease and double-line a 23 cm (9 in) round cake tin.

2   Mix the dried fruit, pineapple and cherries with the flour, spices, ground almonds and chopped nuts.

3   In a separate bowl mix together the melted butter and sugar until pale and fluffy, then mix in the treacle and syrup. Add the beaten eggs, a little at a time. If the mixture looks like it is starting to curdle, add a tablespoon of the flour mixture.

4   Now add half the flour and fruit mixture, stir and fold in the rest. Pour into your prepared tin and spread out to the sides.

5   Bake in the middle shelf of the oven for about 1–1½ hours then reduce the heat to 150°C/300°F/gas 2 and cook for a further 2–2½ hours. Test with a skewer. If it is clean take the cake out of the oven and leave to cool in the tin.

6   If you like you can prick the cake with a fine skewer and slowly pour over 2 to 3 tbsp brandy. To store, wrap in greaseproof paper and put in an airtight tin or cover entirely with aluminium foil.

Blueberry and banana muffins

I like to tell myself that these are a healthy treat as they are packed with fruit. Ideal as a teatime snack or even for breakfast.

PREP TIME 10 minutes
COOKING TIME 20 minutes
MAKES 12

125 g (4½ oz) butter
75 g (3 oz) caster sugar
2 eggs
125 g (4½ oz) plain flour
1½ tsp baking powder
1 tsp vanilla essence
100 g (3½ oz) fresh
   blueberries
1 small banana, chopped

1 Preheat the oven to 180°C/350°F/gas 4.

2 Beat together the butter and sugar and then add the beaten eggs and a tablespoon of the flour (you can do all of this in a food processor). Mix until well combined.

3 Add the rest of the flour, baking powder and a few drops of vanilla essence and mix well. Gently fold in the blueberries and chopped banana.

4 Spoon the mixture into muffin cases, filling to about half way up. Bake in the oven for 15–20 minutes, or until golden and firm to the touch.

Sundried tomato bread with caramelized onions

Making bread is really not that difficult and once you start I guarantee you'll be experimenting with all kinds of different flavours and combinations.

PREP TIME 30 minutes,
  plus rising
COOKING TIME 35 minutes
SERVES 2 round loaves
  about 15 cm (6 in) in
  diameter

2 tbsp olive oil
1 medium onion, thinly sliced
1 tbsp brown sugar
425 g (15 oz) strong bread flour,
  plus extra for dusting
1 tsp salt
3 tbsp sundried tomato paste
1 tbsp fresh oregano, finely
  chopped
7 g (¼ oz) quick-action
  dried yeast
250 ml (9 fl oz) warm water
50 g (2 oz) sundried tomatoes,
  drained and finely chopped
sea salt, for sprinkling

1 First caramelize the onions. Heat the oil in a large pan over a medium heat. Add the onions and cook, stirring frequently for about 10 minutes, or until golden brown. Sprinkle over some brown sugar and cook for a further 2–3 minutes, stirring often. The onions should be dark brown and soft. Remove them from the heat and set aside to cool.

2 Put the flour, salt and tomato paste into a large mixing bowl. Add the chopped oregano and yeast and pour in the warm water.

3 Mix with your hands until the mixture comes together to make a good dough ball. Tip the dough out onto a lightly floured surface and stretch and knead for about 8–10 minutes until the dough is smooth and elastic.

4 Divide the dough into two and add half the onions and sun-dried tomatoes to one piece. Roughly knead into the dough and then shape into a round shape. Sprinkle a little more flour over the top and push your fingers into the dough to create indentations. Repeat to make a second loaf. Place the breads on a baking sheet lined with greaseproof paper and leave to rise for 1 hour in a warm place.

5 When you are ready to bake, drizzle with a little oil (the reserved oil from the sundried tomatoes is ideal) and then cook in a preheated oven at 200°C/400°F/gas 6 for about 35 minutes until golden. Sprinkle with a few flakes of sea salt to serve.

Wayne's Italian breadsticks

Inspired from a cookery course I sent him on, Wayne now makes these bread sticks (and variations of them) whenever we have friends round for a meal. They are a great nibble and go particularly well with homemade soup.

PREP TIME 20 minutes, plus rising
COOKING TIME 10–15 minutes
MAKES about 16 breadsticks

500 g (1 lb 2 oz) strong white bread flour
1 tsp caster sugar
2 tsp salt
7 g (¼ oz) quick-action dried yeast
2 tbsp olive oil
300 ml (10 fl oz) lukewarm water
sea salt, for sprinkling

1 Sieve the flour, sugar, salt and yeast together into a large mixing bowl. Drizzle over the olive oil and make a well in the centre. Pour about half the warm water into the centre and start mixing vigorously, then add the remaining water until you have a sticky dough.

2 Knead for about 8 minutes until the dough is smooth and elastic, then form into a round ball and use a knife to cut a cross on the top. Now place in a lightly oiled bowl and cover with a lightly oiled piece of cling film. Leave in a warm area (if you have an airing cupboard this is the perfect place) to double in size for about an hour.

3 Preheat the oven to 240°C/475°F/gas 9. Divide the dough in half and then shape each half into approximately 8 breadsticks. Place them on a lined baking tray and repeat with the other half of the dough. Carefully brush them with cold water and sprinkle with sea salt.

4 Place them in the oven about bake for 10–15 minutes.

Try flavouring these with fresh rosemary – simply remove and chop the leaves from one sprig of rosemary and roll the breadsticks in the herbs before baking.

Cheese scones

This is a really quick and tasty recipe for cheese scones. They are perfect almost any time of day and are best served slightly warm with butter. Try adding a few snipped chives or some finely chopped fresh thyme to the mixture, before adding the milk.

PREP TIME 10 minutes
COOKING TIME 15 minutes
MAKES about 12

225 g (8 oz) self-raising flour
pinch of salt
55 g (2 oz) butter
55 g (2 oz) mature cheddar, grated
150 ml (5 fl oz) milk

1 Preheat the oven to 200°C/400°F/gas 6.

2 Place the flour, salt and butter in large mixing bowl and use your fingers to blend the ingredients together, until you have something that resembles fine breadcrumbs. Alternatively pulse the ingredients in a food processor.

3 Add the grated cheese and mix to combine. Add the milk gradually and mix until you have a soft dough.

4 Place the dough on a lightly floured surface and stretch and knead. Pat out to a round about 2.5 cm (1 in) thick.

5 Use cutters (round or shaped) to cut out shapes. Place them on a baking sheet. Remember not to waste the scraps – knead them together to make another couple of scones. Brush over the tops of the scones with a little milk and bake for 12–15 minutes until golden.

Party time

Parties can be chaotic as well as fun and with young children you often have to cater for lots of different tastes. In this chapter you will find our favourite party dishes but there are so many other things you can do and you'll find other recipes in the rest of the book that I'm sure will become party favourites. Most of the dishes here are for kids' parties but there are things that adults will enjoy too – just make sure the kids get a look in!

PERFECT PARTY PLANNING

There's nothing to fear from kids' parties! The trick is to be well prepared but you also have to go with the flow – I've found that life with young children is pretty unpredictable! Okay, so something might get spilled, there may be a fight over the last fairy cake and invariably someone cries at the end (let's just hope it's not you). Keep it as simple as possible and follow these survival tips and you should all have a great time.

Food

- Make sure you have some cold food that can be prepared in advance as well as hot dishes.

- Make sandwiches more interesting by using one slice of brown bread and one slice of white and then cutting into strips or even using cutters to make shapes. Vary the fillings so everyone is happy – egg mayonnaise, ham with cream cheese and cucumber and cheese and tomato are all good options.

- Include some healthy options such as carrot, red pepper and baby corn dipping sticks – serve with hummus or a cream cheese and chive dip.

- Fruity jelly makes a great party pud (see page 187).

- Try to avoid crisps – they are packed with salt and fat.

- Relax the rules on sweet treats – its' a party after all! Try the golden crispies (page 188) and chocolate-dipped strawberries (page 191) are some of our party favourites.

- Have plenty of jugs of drink so you can top up throughout the day but avoid fizzy drinks. I usually have a fruity squash drink or some juice diluted with a bit of water.

Entertainment

Unless you're going for the children's entertainer option you'll need to have a few games up your sleeve. Of course it depends on the age of your children but traditional games such as pass the parcel, musical statues and pin the tail on the donkey always go down well. For summer parties try and organize a few outside games – children love treasure hunts and they are great for getting everyone out of the way while you prepare a few last minute dishes.

Decoration

With just a few simple ideas you can really transform a room (or garden) into a party wonderland.

- I love colourful bunting and drape it just about anywhere.

- Fairy lights dotted around a room add instant twinkle and sparkle.

- Kids love balloons – just make sure you have enough to give one to everyone when they leave.

- Use disposable plates and cups or funky plastic picnic ware – they look great and you'll avoid breakages too!

Smoked salmon blinis

These are great as a pre-lunch canapé or as part of a bigger party spread.

PREP TIME 10 minutes
COOKING TIME about
   10 minutes
MAKES about 24

2 x 100 g (3 ½ oz) packets
   mini blinis
120 g (4 oz) crème fraîche
2 tbsp creamed horseradish
freshly ground black pepper
200 g (7 oz) smoked salmon
lemon wedges
dill sprigs, to garnish

1 Preheat the oven to warm the blinis – you can serve them cold but I like to heat them up. Follow the instructions on the packet.

2 Mix together the crème fraîche, horseradish and black pepper and cut the smoked salmon into thin strips.

3 When you are ready to assemble spoon a little of the horseradish cream on to the blinis and then curl a piece of smoked salmon on top. Squeeze over some fresh lemon juice and add a sprig of dill to each one.

If you're not a fan of dill, try snipping a few chives into the crème fraîche instead.

Vegetable party rice

This dish is cooked by the water absorption method. Panch pooran is a delicious Asian spice mix which can be found in any Asian food shop or good supermarket. The name means 'five spices' – usually fenugreek seeds, nigella seeds, mustard seeds, fennel seeds and cumin seeds. You can make your own by mixing up equal quantities of these spices.

PREP TIME 15 minutes
COOKING TIME 20 minutes
SERVES about 6

340 g (12 oz) basmati rice
2 tbsp panch pooran
1 tbsp vegetable oil
1 medium onion, peeled
   and finely chopped
1 vegetable stock cube
120 ml (4 fl oz) coconut milk
340 g (12 oz) mixed vegetables
   (baby corn, mangetout,
   green beans)
1 red pepper, deseeded
   and diced
1 Scotch Bonnet pepper

1 Wash the rice, by swirling the rice with your hand in a bowl of water. Change the water and repeat until the water is clear. Drain in a sieve.

2 Dry-fry the panch pooran until the mustard seeds start to pop. Remove from the pan and set aside. Heat the oil in a large pan and fry the onions until they are translucent. Then crumble in the stock cube.

3 Add the rice, coconut milk, roasted panch pooran, onion and stock cube mix and 900 ml (1 ¾ pints) cold water. Bring to the boil, cover and reduce the heat. Simmer for about 10 minutes.

4 Prepare your chosen vegetables: quarter the baby corn lengthways, trim and halve the mangetout and green beans. When you can see grains of rice over most of the surface of the water in the saucepan, add the vegetables and diced bell pepper, stir and place the Scotch Bonnet pepper on top of the rice and cover.

5 Turn down the heat wait three or four minutes and switch off the heat. The latent heat will complete the cooking of the dish. Gently remove the Scotch Bonnet pepper before serving. Do not burst the pepper!

Cheese twists

These are popular with children and adults alike and are really easy to make. The perfect party nibble!

PREP TIME 15 minutes
COOKING TIME 15 minutes
MAKES about 20

450 g (1 lb) packet of puff
   pastry
2 tbsp grainy mustard
75 g (3 oz) Parmesan,
   grated
2 tbsp poppy seeds

1 Preheat the oven to 220°C/425°F/gas 7. Roll out the pastry on a floured work surface and trim into a square approximately 30 x 30 cm (12 x 12 in).

2 Spread the mustard over the surface and scatter over the grated Parmesan. Fold the pastry in half and lightly roll again.

3 Cut the pastry into long, thin strips about 15 cm (6 in) long. Sprinkle the poppy seeds over the strips and then twist each one into a spiral shape.

4 Place the twists on baking sheets and bake in the oven for 10–15 minutes, or until golden and crisp.

Sticky sausages on sticks

We love nothing more at a party than sausages on sticks. Now, I realize that this is pretty standard party fare but here is a fabulous way to make your sausages a little more special. I promise you they only take 5 minutes to prepare!

PREP TIME 5 minutes
COOKING TIME 40 minutes
SERVES about 15

4 tbsp runny honey
6 tbsp hoisin sauce
   (a delicate barbecue sauce
   also works)
1 tsp white mustard seeds
1 tsp sesame seeds
900 g (2 lb) good-quality
   chipolatas

1   Preheat the oven to 200°C/400°F/gas 6. Place your honey, hoisin sauce, mustard seeds and sesame seeds in a large shallow bowl and mix to combine.

2   Unless you have bought cocktail sausages, you'll need to divide up your chipolatas. Twist each one in the middle and cut in half. Add them to the sticky mixture. When you are happy that all the sausages have a good coverage, tip the sausages and the sauce into a roasting tin lined with foil and cook in the oven for 30–40 minutes, turning occasionally.

3   Serve them on a nice big plate with a shot glass of cocktail sticks waiting at the side. These are delicious served warm or cold but be careful not to serve them straight from the oven. Keep an eye on any greedy grown-ups that might be hovering in the kitchen – you don't want half the sausages to disappear before you've served them!

Party snacks on sticks

These party snacks are a far cry from the kitsch 70s pineapple and cheese cocktail sticks. But kids do love little snacks on sticks and by varying the ingredients you can make them more interesting. Try serving in a halved melon (you can use the melon to make fruit sticks).

PREP TIME 10 minutes

Savoury snacks

halved cherry tomatoes
cucumber slices
cheese cubes (cheddar is a
    favourite but try other
    varieties too)
rolled slices of ham or
    turkey

Serve with a selection of dips such as hummus, mayonnaise or yogurt with chopped fresh mint.

Fruity snacks

strawberries (halved if
    necessary)
seedless white grapes
apple chunks
watermelon or melon chunks

Serve with a selection of dips such as Greek yogurt swirled with honey or melted chocolate.

Fresh fruit red berry jellies

There is no denying how much kids love jelly. Try this great recipe for a healthy party food packed with lots of fresh fruit. It's so simple you can tailor it to your own child's tastes and create many different versions as there is so much fruit to choose from. Watch out for some fruits – kiwis and pineapple contain an enzyme that prevents the gelatine from setting so are probably best avoided.

PREP TIME 5 minutes, plus chilling
SERVES 4

600 ml (1 pint) fresh orange juice
4 sheets of leaf gelatine
75 g (3 oz) strawberries, hulled and quartered
50 g (2 oz) raspberries
25 g (1 oz) redcurrants

1 Pour the orange juice into a bowl and add the sheets of gelatine. Dissolve in a microwave for about 30 seconds. Alternatively, heat the orange juice in a bowl over a pan of boiling water and stir in the gelatine until it has dissolved. Allow to cool.

2 Divide the fruit equally between four pretty serving bowls (glass ones work really well) and pour over the orange juice. Chill in the fridge for at least 2 hours or until set (this is a good recipe to do in the advance – the night before if necessary).

Golden crispies

Mum's rice crispie cakes were a must for all of our birthday parties and I used to love helping her make them – easy and delicious.

PREP TIME 10 minutes
MAKES about 16

75 g (3 oz) rice crispies or cornflakes
4 tbsp golden syrup
1 tbsp sugar
15 g (½ oz) butter
few drops of vanilla essence

1 Lightly grease and then line a 20 cm (8 in) square baking tray with greaseproof paper.

2 Put your syrup, sugar and butter into a saucepan and heat gently until the butter has melted and all the sugar has dissolved.

3 Allow to cool slightly and then add the vanilla essence and the rice crispies or cornflakes. Mix thoroughly.

4 Turn into your prepared tin and press down well. Leave to cool and then chill in the refrigerator. When you are ready to serve, cut the crispies into squares and serve in pretty cake cases.

Chocolate-dipped strawberries

This is such a simple idea but is always a huge hit. They look really pretty served on a lovely big platter.

PREP TIME 15 minutes,
  plus chilling
SERVES about 12

450 g (1 lb) strawberries
100 g (4 oz) milk chocolate
  drops
100 g (4 oz) white chocolate
  drops

1 Hull and wash your strawberries under a running cold tap in a colander. Tip them onto a piece of kitchen towel and pat gently with another piece, spread them out and leave to dry.

2 Bring a saucepan of water to the boil and then remove it from the heat. Put the milk chocolate and white chocolate in two separate bowls and carefully place one of them inside the pan. Use a spoon to stir until all the chocolate has melted. Repeat with the other bowl of chocolate (you may need to reheat the water).

3 Lay a piece of parchment paper on a baking sheet. Dip your strawberries into the chocolate. I think it's best if the chocolate covers around a half of the fruit. Make sure it drips over the chocolate bowl and not your plate, then place them on the paper. Now place them in your fridge for around 20 minutes to set.

4 Finally you can gently peel the strawberries of the paper and place them on a serving platter.

Tip
This would also work well with clementine segments.

White chocolate and marshmallow squares

A great homemade treat for the kids to nibble on...

PREP TIME 15 minutes, plus chilling
MAKES about 16 squares

40 g (1½ oz) white chocolate drops
80 g (3 oz) rice crispies
80 g (3 oz) white marshmallows
25 g (1 oz) butter

1 Lightly grease and base line a 20 cm (8 in) square cake tin with some greaseproof paper.

2 Mix the chocolate drops in with the rice crispies and set aside. You can chop the white chocolate drops up if you think they are too large.

3 Roughly chop the marshmallows and place in a large saucepan with the butter. Cook over a low heat until it has all melted, stirring gently. This should take about 5 minutes.

4 Remove from the heat and stir in the rice crispies and chocolate mix until well combined. Transfer to your baking tin and place in the fridge for a couple of hours.

5 To turn it out, loosen around the edges and then flip onto a chopping board. Peel off the paper and cut into squares.

Cranberry fizz

This is a lovely fruity drink that children will love too – it's a bit more grown up than the usual squash that they get at most parties. Simple and delicious.

PREP TIME 2 minutes
SERVES 8

ice cubes
1.2 litres (2 pints) chilled
    cranberry juice
600 ml (1 pint) chilled
    lemonade
juice of 1 lemon
raspberries or redcurrants,
    to garnish

1 Fill tall glasses up to a third with ice cubes and then pour in the cranberry juice until the glasses are about three-quarters full.

2 Top up with lemonade and then squeeze over the fresh lemon juice. Stir and add the redcurrants for a pretty garnish. You could also pop in a couple of fresh raspberries. Serve with coloured straws.

Try freezing grapes and then using them as ice cubes. You can eat them too – they are a bit like eating instant grape sorbet!

Hot mulled apple juice

My cousin Dave has inspired many culinary delights in this book but he also turns up every now and then with some great drink recipes. This is the perfect drink for Halloween or bonfire night parties – and if you want an alcoholic version, just replace the apple juice with a quality cider.

PREP TIME 10 minutes
COOKING TIME 25 minutes
SERVES 6–8

1.5 litres (2½ pints) pressed
   apple juice
500 ml (¾ pint) water
55 g (2 oz) brown sugar
1 cinnamon stick
2 apples, cored and sliced

For the spice bag
1 tbsp whole cloves
1 tbsp allspice
good pinch of nutmeg
1 lemon, rind peeled

1 First make your spice bag. Cut a square of fine muslin and place the spices and lemon rind in the centre (reserve the lemon for later). Tie up tightly.

2 Place the apple juice and water in a large pan and bring gently to the boil. Add the spice bag, sugar and juice of the lemon. Cover and simmer for about 20 minutes.

3 Remove from the heat and add the cinnamon stick and apple slices. Allow to cool slightly before serving.

Raspberry and elderflower Bellini

This is a little something for the adults – it's a perfect aperitif or summer drink to enjoy while the kids are running round the garden. Prosecco is what would be used in an authentic Italian version but you could use champagne or another good-quality sparkling wine.

PREP TIME 5 minutes
SERVES 6

juice of 1 lemon
12 chilled raspberries
6 tsp elderflower cordial
1 bottle chilled Prosecco or
   other sparkling wine

1   Place a couple of raspberries, a squeeze of lemon juice and 1 teaspoon of elderflower cordial into each champagne flute. You can prepare this bit in advance.

2   Pour chilled Prosecco into each glass and serve immediately.

Trying new things

Most children I know (including my own) go through a 'funny food' phase – suddenly everything has to be plain and things that they used to like get pushed around the plate and left to get cold. It's hard not to get frustrated but most children grow out of these irrational fears. I've been quite lucky with my three as they are usually quite willing to try things. I've found that involving them in shopping and preparing food really helps but making things a bit more fun is a good idea too. The recipes in this chapter are quite varied – some of them have a little bit more spice in them while others use more unusual ingredients or flavour combinations.

Stir-fried vegetables

Stir-fries are so quick and simple to make and are great for making sure your children get a good variety of vegetables. The other good thing is that you can add or leave out whatever vegetables you and the family want – although I sometimes sneak in new ingredients that I'm keen for the kids to try! The sesame oil gives the dish a lovely authentic Asian flavour.

PREP TIME 5 minutes
COOKING TIME 15 minutes
SERVES 4–6

For the sauce
1 tbsp soy sauce
2 tbsp peanut butter
2.5 cm (1 in) piece fresh ginger, peeled and finely chopped
1 garlic clove, peeled and crushed
pinch of salt

1 tbsp vegetable oil
½ red pepper, deseeded and sliced
½ green pepper, deseeded and sliced
50 g (2 oz) mushrooms, sliced
50 g (2 oz) baby sweetcorn
50 g (2 oz) sugar-snap peas
½ red onion, peeled and sliced
1 carrot, peeled and cut into batons
1 courgette, cut into batons
50 g (2 oz) beansprouts
25 g (1 oz) cashew nuts
25 g (1 oz) pumpkin seeds
25 g (1 oz) peanuts
1 tbsp sesame oil (optional)

1 First make the sauce. Simply place all the ingredients together in a bowl and mix until you have a thick paste.

2 Heat the oil in a wok or large frying pan. Add the peppers, mushrooms, sweetcorn, sugar-snap peas, onion, carrot and courgette and cook over a high heat for 3 minutes.

3 Add the beansprouts, cashew nuts, pumpkin seeds and peanuts and the paste. Cook for a further 2 minutes, stirring so that the paste is worked into the vegetables. I try not to overcook as the vegetables taste best if they are crunchy when eaten.

4 Drizzle over the sesame oil (if using) and serve straight away, either with some plain rice or noodles or as an accompaniment to grilled fish or chicken.

Tips

If you are using toasted sesame oil use half the amount as it has a much stronger flavour.

If you want you can also add chicken – simply add strips of chicken to the wok before adding the vegetables. Cook for about 6–8 minutes or until just cooked through.

Granny's tomato sambal

My Granny brought many wonderful recipes back from India and this sambal has been created in our family hundreds of times ever since. It is a great accompaniment to lots of different dishes but Wayne and I love it spread on to thick slices of toast. Beware, it has quite a kick!

PREP TIME 5 minutes
COOKING TIME 15 minutes
SERVES about 4

1 tbsp olive oil
1 large red onion, peeled
  and chopped
½ tsp cayenne pepper
½ tsp ground turmeric
1 x 400 g (14 oz) tin chopped
  tomatoes
½ tsp sugar
1 tbsp balsamic or red wine
  vinegar

1 Heat the oil in a pan and fry the onion until soft and golden, about 5 minutes.

2 Add the cayenne pepper and ground turmeric and cook for 1–2 minutes; then add the chopped tomatoes.

3 Add the sugar and vinegar and continue to cook for about 5–10 minutes. Serve with grilled sausages or a piece of grilled fish or just use to dunk some fresh bread into.

Curried parsnip soup

This one is so tasty – the sweetness of the parsnip together with the curry flavours combine so well. Serve with a chunk of granary bread.

PREP TIME 25 minutes
COOKING TIME 50 minutes
SERVES 4

40 g (1½ oz) butter
1 onion, peeled and choped
675 g (1½ lb) parsnips, peeled
   and finely diced
2 tsp curry powder
½ tsp ground cumin
1½ litres (2½ pints) chicken
   stock
150 ml (5 fl oz) single cream
salt and freshly ground
   black pepper
pinch ground paprika,
   to garnish

1 Heat the butter in a large pan and fry the onion and diced parsnip over a medium heat for about 3 minutes.

2 Stir in the curry powder and ground cumin and cook for a further 2 minutes. Add the chicken stock and bring to the boil. Lower the heat, cover and simmer for about 45 minutes until the vegetables are tender.

3 Allow to cool slightly, then using a slotted spoon, transfer the vegetables to a blender or food processor. Add a little of the stock and then purée until smooth. Return to the pan. Alternatively use a hand-held blender.

4 Add the cream and season to taste. Reheat to serving temperature but do not boil. Serve sprinkled with paprika.

Fish kebabs

This is a good way to try out different kinds of fish on your kids and is really healthy too. You can cook this under a hot grill or on a barbecue. Serve with a nice green salad. For an extra kick, try using chilli oil instead of olive oil in the marinade.

PREP TIME 10 minutes
COOKING TIME 5 minutes
SERVES 4

250 g (9 oz) raw king
   prawns, peeled
300 g (10 oz) tuna steak,
   cut into chunks
300 g (10 oz) skinless and
   boneless salmon fillet,
   cut into chunks
1 lemon, quartered
1 lime, quartered

For the marinade
1 garlic clove, peeled and
   crushed
2 tbsp olive oil
2 tbsp teriyaki sauce
juice of ½ lime

1 Soak 4 long wooden skewers in a bowl of water for about 30 minutes to prevent them burning on the grill or barbecue.

2 Put the marinade ingredients in a large bowl and mix well to combine. Add the prawns and fish and gently coat in the marinade. Cover and leave to marinate in the refrigerator for at least one hour.

3 Thread the fish and prawns onto the skewers, starting with a piece of lime and ending with a piece of lemon. Grill the kebabs under a hot grill for approximately 4–5 minutes, turning once and brushing with the marinade to prevent burning.

Easy Thai green curry

Uncle Dave's curry has been a huge hit in the family and – to our surprise – very popular with the children. We do go a bit easy on the curry paste to make it more palatable for them. If you are making this for adults you can experiment with the paste and oyster sauce to give it much more of a kick. We actually cook this with quorn most of the time.

PREP TIME 10 minutes
COOKING TIME 20 minutes
SERVES 4

1 tbsp olive oil
4 skinless chicken breasts, cut into chunks
1 tbsp Thai green curry paste
1 x 400 ml (14 fl oz) tin coconut milk
½ tsp oyster sauce
50 g (2 oz) baby corn, sliced into rounds
100 g (3½ oz) broccoli, cut into small florets
50 g (2 oz) mangetout
75 g (3 oz) button or chestnut mushrooms, quartered

To serve
basmati rice
fresh bay leaves

1 Heat the oil in a large pan or wok and sear the chicken over a medium to high heat until browned on all sides. Add the curry paste and cook for a further 2 minutes. Resist the temptation to add extra curry paste (unless you know you really like it spicy) as it has quite a kick – you can always add more later.

2 Add the coconut milk, and bring to the boil. Reduce the heat to a simmer and cook for a further 10 minutes. Meanwhile cook the basmati rice according to the packet instructions. I like to add one or two fresh bay leaves to the pan to give the rice a subtle flavour.

3 Add the oyster sauce to the curry and then add in the baby corn, broccoli, mangetout and mushrooms. Cook for a further 3–4 minutes depending on how you like the vegetables. Serve immediately in pretty bowls with the basmati rice.

Chicken paprika

This is another dish that we all love to eat in our family. It's not that spicy – just delicious and flavoursome. Serve with rice or noodles.

PREP TIME 20 minutes
COOKING TIME 55 minutes
SERVES 6

4–6 skinless chicken breasts
3 tbsp olive oil
2 onions, peeled and chopped
1 green pepper, deseeded
   and cut into strips
1 red pepper, deseeded and
   cut into strips
2 tbsp plain flour
400 ml (14 fl oz) chicken
   stock
1 tbsp paprika
1 tbsp tomato purée
½ tsp sugar
salt and freshly ground
   black pepper
75 ml (3 fl oz) single cream
2 tbsp chopped fresh parsley

1 Preheat the oven to 180°C/350°F/gas 4. Cut the chicken into strips.

2 Heat the oil in a large frying pan add the chicken strips. Cook for about 3–4 minutes until browned on all sides. Transfer to a lidded casserole dish.

3 Add the onions to pan and cook for about 3 minutes until transparent. Add the peppers and cook for a further 2 minutes. Stir in the flour and cook for 1 minute, then slowly add the stock, stirring constantly until the sauce bubbles and thickens.

4 Add the paprika, tomato purée and sugar and season to taste. Pour the sauce over the chicken, cover and cook in the oven for about 45 minutes or until the chicken is tender. Stir in the cream just before serving and sprinkle with the chopped parsley.

Lemon soup

This delicious and unusual sounding soup is a recipe from our good friend Howard's mum, who lives on the Greek island of Rhodes. Serve with freshly toasted pitta breads, cut into triangles.

PREP TIME 5 minutes
COOKING TIME 25 minutes
SERVES 4

1.4 litres (2½ pints) chicken stock
200 g (7 oz) long-grain rice
2 eggs
juice of 1 lemon
salt and freshly ground black pepper
2 tbsp chopped fresh parsley

1 Place the chicken stock and rice in a large pan and bring to the boil. Cover and simmer until the rice is just tender – this should take about 20 minutes.

2 Meanwhile, beat the eggs in a mixing bowl and whisk in the lemon juice. Add a little of the hot stock to the egg mixture and whisk well; then slowly pour the eggs into the hot (but not boiling) soup, stirring constantly.

3 Add the salt and black pepper to taste and another tablespoon of lemon juice if necessary. Pour into serving bowls and sprinkle with the chopped parsley.

Pork chops with apples and pears

Cooking pork with apples is a classic combination – the tartness of the fruit really works well with the meat. Adding pears as well gives it a little twist.

PREP TIME 10 minutes
COOKING TIME 15 minutes
SERVES 2

1 tbsp of olive oil
25 g (1 oz) butter
1 garlic glove, finely chopped
2 pork chops, trimmed of
   excess fat
1 tsp brown sugar
1 apple, cored and thinly
   sliced
1 pear, cored and thinly sliced
1 tbsp Dijon mustard
100 ml (3½ fl oz) cider

1 Heat the oil and half the butter in a large heavy-based frying pan until sizzling. Add the garlic and then the chops and brown on both sides. Cook gently for about 5 minutes on each side. Remove the chops from the pan and keep warm.

2 Add the rest of the butter to the pan and sprinkle in the brown sugar. Add the apples and pears to the pan. Sauté the fruit for a couple of minutes until it just starts to soften.

3 Add the mustard and the cider to the pan and bring to the boil. Allow to bubble for a few minutes and then return the chops to the pan for a couple of minutes.

4 Serve each chop with the fruit piled on top and the sauce drizzled over. Perfect with creamy mashed potatoes and green vegetables.

Chicken with limes

Chicken thighs are a cheaper alternative to chicken breasts and I personally think they taste much better (there is more flavour in the darker meat). There is quite a lot of spice in this dish – you can omit the chillies if you prefer but I think it's great to introduce children to all the wonderful flavours out there. Serve this with Granny's tomato sambal (see page 203).

PREP TIME 15 minutes
COOKING TIME 1 hour
SERVES 6

1.5 kg (3½ lb) chicken thighs
2 tbsp vegetable oil
2 garlic cloves, peeled and
   chopped
1 small onion, peeled and
   finely chopped
½ tsp turmeric
2 tsp ground coriander
2 tsp ground cumin
2–3 fresh chillies, deseeded
   and finely chopped
1 tsp chilli powder
2 tbsp soy sauce
salt and freshly ground
   black pepper
3 limes

1   Preheat the oven to 190°C/375°F/gas 5. Rinse the chicken and pat dry with kitchen paper. You can remove the skin if you prefer but I like to keep it on.

2   Heat the oil in a pan and brown the chicken thighs on both sides. Remove from the pan and set aside. Add the garlic and onion and fry for about 5 minutes, until soft and golden.

3   Add the turmeric, coriander, cumin, chillies, chilli powder, soy sauce and salt and pepper. Cook, stirring, for about 2 minutes.

4   Place the chicken thighs in a casserole dish and spoon over the onion and spice mixture. Squeeze the juice from 2 limes over the chicken, cover and cook in the oven for about 45 minutes.

5   Serve garnished with the remaining lime, cut into wedges.

Tabbouleh

Originally from Lebanon, but now popular throughout the Middle East, tabbouleh is a salad made from bulghur wheat. Don't confuse bulghur wheat with cracked wheat, which is very hard and takes longer to cook. Similar to couscous, bulghur wheat can be found in most good supermarkets, health food shops and delis. This is a really excellent high-fibre food and is great served with flatbreads or toasted pitta. You could also try using lettuce leaves to scoop it up – little gem leaves work well for this.

PREP TIME 15 minutes
COOKING TIME 10 minutes
SERVES 6

150 g (5 oz) bulghur wheat
2–3 large ripe tomatoes, quartered (some people remove the cores but I just leave them as they are)
1 large bunch of flat-leaf parsley, finely chopped
1 small handful fresh mint leaves, finely chopped
2 spring onions, finely chopped
5 tbsp extra-virgin olive oil
juice of 1 lemon
salt and freshly ground black pepper to taste
bread and lettuce leaves, to serve
yogurt dip, to serve

1 Cook the bulghur wheat according to the packet instructions, then drain well. Transfer to a large serving bowl.

2 Dice the tomatoes and add to the bulghur wheat with the parsley, mint and chopped spring onions.

3 Whisk together the olive oil and lemon juice and season to taste. Pour over the bulghur wheat and stir through.

4 To serve pile the tabbouleh onto a large serving dish lined with lettuce leaves and some warm bread and olives on the side. You could also whizz up a really simple yogurt dip, just add one crushed garlic clove, 1 finely chopped cucumber and some chopped mint to about 400 ml (14 fl oz) plain yogurt and mix together.

Sautéed aubergine and tomatoes with a minted yogurt dip

This is a lovely main course for a summer supper and will be hit even for non-veggies! If you want to make it a more substantial meal, serve with some sliced grilled halloumi cheese.

PREP TIME 20 minutes
COOKING TIME 10 minutes
SERVES 2

1 large aubergine
4 tbsp olive oil
120 g (4 oz) vine-ripened
   cherry tomatoes, halved
1 garlic clove, finely chopped
   or crushed
1 shallot, finely chopped
salt and freshly ground black
   pepper
125 ml (4 fl oz) natural yogurt
1 tbsp chopped fresh mint
juice of ½ lemon
mint leaves, to garnish

1 Cut the aubergine lengthways into about 6 thick slices. Brush each slice with a little oil on both sides.

2 Heat the remaining oil over a medium heat in a small pan and add the tomatoes, garlic and shallot. Cook gently for 3–4 minutes until the tomatoes are just beginning to soften. Season to taste and remove from the heat.

3 Cook the aubergine slices under a medium hot grill for about 5 minutes on each side, until they are nicely softened. Alternatively if you have a griddle pan you can cook them by heating up the pan and then adding the slices, cooking for about 3 minutes on each side.

4 In a small bowl mix together the yogurt, mint, lemon juice and season to taste.

5 Arrange 2 or 3 slices of aubergine on a plate with a generous dollop of the minty dip on each and the sautéed tomatoes on the side. Garnish with mint leaves and serve with some delicious warm bread.

Traditional Welsh cawl

This wonderful broth recipe has come from Wayne's Nana Mildred. This is a hugely popular recipe in Wales and a perfect way to give the children a bowl full of pure goodness. There are no major rules on what vegetables you use – cawl is often made with whatever you have in your fridge that week. However, for it to be called cawl it has to have the leeks – I'm told in no uncertain terms.

PREP TIME 15 minutes
COOKING TIME 2½ hours
SERVES 6

2 tbsp vegetable oil
1–1.4 kg (2–3 lb) best end
    Welsh lamb neck cutlets,
    trimmed of excess fat
1 lamb stock cube
salt and freshly ground
    black pepper
1 large onion, peeled and
    sliced
2 large carrots, sliced
1 medium parsnip, cut into
    chunks
2 white turnips, peeled
    and cut into chunks
3 leeks
6 small potatoes, peeled
2 tbsp chopped parsley

1 Heat the oil in a pan and brown the lamb on all sides. Remove from the pan and place the cutlets in a large casserole. Cover with cold water (about 2 litres/4 pints) and add the stock cube. Season with salt and pepper. Bring to the boil and simmer slowly for 1 hour.

2 Remove from the heat and allow to cool slightly before skimming the fat off the surface. Return to the heat and add the onion, carrots, parsnip, turnips and two of the leeks, thickly sliced. Cover and cook on a very low simmer for another hour.

3 Halve the potatoes, add to the pan and cook for a further 20 minutes. Finely chop the remaining leek and add to the pan with the chopped parsley. Cook for a further 5 minutes.

4 Some families would serve this in the style of a French 'pot-au-feu' – which is when the broth is served first, followed by the meat and vegetables as a second course.

Index

Acknowledgements

I would like to thank the following very special people. Creating a book like this would not have been possible without their love, support and inspiration. Oh, and their recipes!

To my Mum, Dad, Warren, Jamie, Granny and Aunty Kath for a wonderful childhood – thank you.

My fantastic friends for some fantastic meals and recipes. Tracy Roberts, Dai Bach, Howard Trigg, David Paris Malham, Sophie and Graham Breakenridge, Beth and Henry Steedman, Jo Philips, Gordon Greenock, Christian Platts, Natalie and Richard Ganpatsingh. Keep them coming! The rest of my family and friends, who have helped or shared some of their delicious recipes. The amazing group of parents and teachers at Alderbridge Steiner-Waldorf School whose creative spark inspires such a wholesome appreciation for the simplest and healthiest food.

My agents Jaine J Brent and Antony Read at Jaine J Brent Creative Management and Branding for the tireless energy, encouragement and constant support they pour into everything I do.

Clare Sayer and all at New Holland, for turning a lifetime's recipes and knowledge into something beautiful to look at and – more importantly – something that readers can use and enjoy. We shared a belief that not all our favourite meals come from the superchefs and their fabulous restaurants but from the lives and the kitchens of us the ordinary folk. Thanks for making this book happen. Tony Briscoe for his beautiful photographs and Jacqui Caulton for her great design.

My wonderful husband Wayne who has given so much thought, time and energy helping me create this book. For the care he puts into mealtimes despite the fact that until we had children he couldn't rustle up beans on toast without incinerating it!

And last, but by no means least, my beautiful children Morgan, Flynn and Evie – the real reason why our mealtimes are filled with love, health and vitality. Your appreciation for home cooked food keeps me motivated and inspired.